wholeperson
Stress & Wellness Publishers

101 W. 2nd St., Suite 203
Duluth, MN 55802

800-247-6789

books@wholeperson.com
www.wholeperson.com

Teens – Accept and Embrace Diversity
Facilitator Reproducible Activities for Groups and Individuals

Printed in the United States of America

10 9 8 7 6 5 4 3 2 1

Editorial Director: Carlene Sippola
Art Director: Joy Morgan Dey

Library of Congress Control Number: 2014909586
ISBN: 978-157025-317-1

Teens ~ Accept and Embrace Diversity
Purpose of the Book

> Nelson Mandela's eloquent words below express the theme of this book.
>
> *No one is born hating another person because of the color of his skin, or his background, or his religion.*
> *People must learn to hate, and if they can learn to hate, they can be taught to love, for love comes more naturally to the human heart than its opposite.*

Exclusion or inclusion, discord or harmony hinge on hating or appreciating cultural differences.

This book is very relevant today because school shootings and teen suicides often relate to being left out, laughed at, and bullied because of cultural differences.

Teens ~ Accept and Embrace Diversity capitalizes on what comes naturally – cohesion not cruelty.

Teens can un-learn bigotry and become broad-minded, experience empathy for people they previously judged and replace criticism with compassion.

To welcome diversity reduces and/or diminishes prejudice and nurtures respect for one's own and others' cultures.

In this book, the word culture pertains to similar behavior, values, beliefs and/or characteristics of a particular group of people and relates to the following common bonds:

- Age
- Body (shape, size and weight)
- Disability
- Ethnicity
- Family
- Gender
- Neighborhood
- Race
- Religion
- Sexual orientation
- Social subcultures
- Spirituality
- Status (financial, cliques, etc.)
- Other common bonds (school, sports team, etc.)

An important exception to acceptance is pop culture's presentation of aggression. Teens are encouraged to debate its possible effects and to create a culture of non-violence via video scripts and performances, song lyrics, posters, bumper stickers, door decorations to identify the connection between anger and depression, and to consider a *media violence diet.*

To embrace diversity is a giant step toward life, and a better quality of life, for potentially marginalized people and for possible perpetrators of prejudice, who focus on becoming promoters of peace.

Teens ~ Accept and Embrace Diversity

Format of the Book

An Introduction for Teen Participants motivates teens for the activities in this book (page vi).

A Cover Page for each chapter provides a motivational quotation and session descriptions. Cover pages may be provided to teens to promote workshops or to introduce a series of sessions.

Seven chapters, four to eighteen sessions per chapter, (total of sixty-two) encompass the following:

1. **Accepting Diversity**
   Diversity definitions and cheers, cultural considerations, assimilation and multiculturalism, chess game and animal analogies, commonalities and closed-minded versus open-minded reactions.
2. **Physical Diversity**
   Prejudice or preference based on appearance, sensitivity toward people with disabilities, disease conditions or sensory impairments. Refute misleading media messages about a *perfect* body.
3. **Mental Diversity**
   Ways to diminish stigmas against people with mental health issues or learning difficulties, to overcome cultural barriers to expressing feelings and seeking help, to dispel myths about mental illness and to recognize everybody has strengths.
4. **Social Diversity**
   Hate and hope, socioeconomic status, gender stereotypes, being an ally – not a bystander, sexual orientation issues, motives underlying bullying and bigotry, and viewing people as multi-dimensional – learning not to categorize them based on one trait.
5. **Exceptions to Acceptance**
   To reject media messages that glamorize aggression and to promote a culture of non-violence through song lyrics, posters, debates, bumper stickers, mock videos, panel discussions, etc.
6. **Avoiding Stereotypes and Prejudice**
   Self-segregation versus inclusion, non-judgmental attitudes, unlearning hate and learning to love, identifying dangers of labels, scapegoating, making false assumptions about fame and failure, facing mob mentality versus individualism, seeking people, places and things that define one's roots, defining reasons not to bully, and studying civil rights quotations and depictions.
7. **Advocacy in Action**
   The difference one person can make, the value of collaborative efforts at home, school, the community and world, personal attributes of an advocate, and ways to use one's talents to *give back to the universe.*

Each chapter may be a workshop or seminar with daily or weekly sessions.
To recruit participants, emphasize the interactive and expressive aspects of activities.

Sessions throughout the book may be mixed and matched, presented in any order and linked to teens' needs and current societal events.

Activities are adaptable for interactive or individual completion.
Most handouts can be experienced independently or with partners or teammates.

Each session includes:
Reproducible handouts for teens: delete with white out, add words, photocopy, cut on broken lines, etc.
For the Facilitator page: on the back of each handout or set of handouts provides …

- I. Purpose – goals for the teens
- II. General Comments – brief background information
- III. Possible Activities – ideas to introduce topics, responses to elicit, answer keys, etc.
- IV. Enrichment Activities – additional learning opportunities and ways to conclude sessions.

Facilitator discretion is suggested as sensitive subjects are addressed.
Facilitators need to be aware to refer teens in crisis for a mental health evaluation or to call 911 or the local emergency service number.

Suggestions for Facilitating

EACH SESSION

Active – expect movement
- Teammates confer
- Volunteers write on the board
- Actors perform role plays, skits, mock videos
- Audience joins in

Collaborative – motivate teens to teach each other
- Game show hosts
- Teammates
- Chairpersons

Comfortable – encourage teens to volunteer as they wish, rather than feeling they must respond

Confidential – "What is said in this room, stays in this room."

Expressive – incorporate a variety of hands-on activities
- Art
- Music
- Drama
- Poetry
- Storytelling

Fun – engage teens in interactive activities
- Songs
- Dances
- Games
- Debates
- Panel Discussions
- Posters
- Presentations
- Video Scripts

Non-threatening – promote safe, honest self-expression

Relevant – help teens to …
- Personalize concepts
- Foster diversity in their hearts, homes, schools and neighborhoods

Risk rewarding – gently persuade teens to …
- Share their work
- Take center stage
- Adopt leadership roles in session
- Act as advocates in real life situations

The ideal facilitator welcomes various viewpoints, is non-judgmental, includes all participants, shows sensitivity to teens with special needs and teaches by example, the ultimate teaching tool.

Teens ~ Accept and Embrace Diversity

Introduction for Participants

Teens ~ Accept and Embrace Diversity
allows you to consider new ways of reacting to cultural differences.

In this book, the word culture pertains to similar behavior, values, beliefs and/or characteristics of a particular group of people:

- age
- body (shape, size and weight)
- disability
- ethnicity
- family
- gender
- neighborhood
- race
- religion
- sexual orientation
- social sub-cultures
- spiritual
- status (financial, cliques, etc.)
- other common bonds (school, sports teams, etc.)

The activities in this book will help you deal with the following items in your teen years and for the rest of your life:

- Differences among people
- Rejection and acceptance
- Ways to include or exclude others
- Bullying and bigotry
- Hate and love
- Being a bystander or an ally
- Judgmental or open-minded attitudes
- The *same old* or a new way

You can set the pace for your involvement:

- Jump in with both feet as a leader or participant
- Take a back seat as an observer
- Test the waters by working with a partner or team
- Dig deep and keep your responses private
- Share your thoughts and feelings

You will be encouraged to accept other cultures' various views and to become aware of the influences of your own home life, environment, friends, community, and media. You will be encouraged to think for yourself.

You may inspire others to take the high road — to love.

Teens – *Accept and Embrace Diversity*

TABLE OF CONTENTS

Our gratitude to the following for their exceptional input ~

Annette Damien, MS, PPS
Beth Jennings, CTEC Counselor
Hannah Lavoie, teenager

And to these professionals who make us look good!

Art Director – Joy Dey
Editor and Lifelong Teacher – Eileen Regen
Editorial Director – Carlene Sippola
Illustrator – Amy L. Brodsky
Proofreader – Jay Leutenberg

ACCEPTING DIVERSITY 1

I know there is strength in the differences between us.
I know there is comfort where we overlap.

~ Ani Di Franco

Diversity Definitions

CULTURE – In this book, culture pertains to similar behavior, values, beliefs and/or characteristics of a particular group of people and may relate to age, body – ideal image, disability, ethnicity, family, gender, neighborhood, race, religion, sexual orientation, social subcultures, spiritual, status or other common bonds.

Acceptance . . . . belief that all people are entitled to be treated equally.

Ageism . . . . prejudice or discrimination based on a particular age.

Bigotry . . . . narrow beliefs based on pre-judgment and views of others.

Body - Ideal Image. . . . an illusion promoted by the media that only a *perfect* body is acceptable.

Classism . . . . prejudice based on economic or social status.

Culture . . . . similar behavior, beliefs and characteristics related by a common bond

Disability. . . . . a long-term physical, mental, intellectual or sensory impairment which in interaction with various barriers may hinder full and effective participation in society on an equal basis with others.

Discrimination . . . . unfair treatment of someone based on cultural differences.

Diversity . . . . different cultures coming together in communities.

Ethnic Group . . . . people of common national origin and/or religion.

Ethnocentrism . . . . . . attitude that one's own culture is superior.

Equality. . . . . rights, treatment, opportunities, value, etc. are fair and the same.

Gender Bias . . . . the differential treatment of men and women based on their gender.

Gender Identity . . . . . . feeling of belonging to a particular sex, regardless of one's anatomical sex traits.

Human Rights . . . . rights that belong to everyone: life, liberty, justice and self-determination in economic, cultural, political, religious, education and employment opportunities, etc.

Inclusion . . . . the addition, presence and acceptance of people in any culture.

Lookism . . . . prejudice based on physical appearance

Prejudice . . . . judgment formed before building sufficient knowledge.

Race . . . . people who share a common descent or heredity.

Racism . . . . belief that race is the primary determinant of traits and capacities which produce superiority of a particular race and inferiority or dehumanization of others.

Religion . . . . the practice of beliefs, ritual observance of faith.

Sexism . . . . attitude, prejudice, stereotyping or discrimination on the basis of gender.

Sexual Orientation. . . . personal experiences, attractions, identification; genetic and gender-associated behaviors.

Social Subcultures. . . . people who interact with one another within a defined culture.

Spirituality . . . . a connected feeling to self and to something larger than self.

Status . . . . the relative position or rank of somebody or something in a society or culture.

Stereotype . . . . a generalized mental picture of a culture based on info/mis-info about a few.

Stigma . . . . a label of disgrace or disapproval imposed by others to spoil identity and isolate persons from the group or society.

Tolerance . . . . non-judgment of another person, situation, ideology or culture.

Xenophobia . . . . fear or hatred of strangers, foreigners, or the unfamiliar.

Diversity Definitions and Meanings Match-Up

WORDS	MEANINGS	
1. **Acceptance**	A. people of common national origin or religion	
2. **Ageism**	B. the differential treatment of men and women based on their gender	
3. **Bigotry**	C. unfair treatment of someone based on cultural differences	
4. **Body – Ideal Image**	D. the addition, presence and acceptance of people in any culture	
5. **Classism**	E. rights, treatment, opportunities, value, etc. are fair and the same	
6. **Culture**	F. rights that belong to everyone: life, liberty, justice and self determination in economic, cultural, political, religious, education and employment opportunities, etc.	
7. **Disability**	G. an illusion promoted by the media that only a *perfect* body is acceptable.	
8. **Discrimination**	H. belief that people are entitled to be treated equally	
9. **Diversity**	I. narrow beliefs based on pre-judgment and views of others	
10. **Ethnic Group**	J. the practice of beliefs, ritual observance of faith	
11. **Ethnocentrism**	K. judgment formed before building sufficient knowledge	
12. **Equality**	L. prejudice or discrimination based on a particular age	
13. **Gender Bias**	M. people who share a common descent or heredity	
14. **Gender Identity**	N. people who interact with one another within a defined culture	
15. **Human Rights**	O. attitude that one's own culture is superior	
16. **Inclusion**	P. a connected feeling to self and to something larger than self	
17. **Lookism**	Q. the relative position or rank of someone or something in a society or culture, i.e., financial, cliques, etc.	
18. **Prejudice**	R. a generalized mental picture of a culture based on info misinformation about a few	
19. **Race**	S. non-judgment of another person, situation, ideology or culture	
20. **Racism**	T. feeling of belonging to a particular sex, regardless of one's anatomical sex traits	
21. **Religion**	U. prejudice based on economic or social status	
22. **Sexism**	V. fear or hatred of strangers, foreigners, or the unfamiliar	
23. **Sexual Orientation**	W. a label of disgrace or disapproval imposed by others to spoil identity and isolate persons from the group or society	
24. **Social Subcultures**	X. different cultures coming together in communities	
25. **Spirituality**	Y. similar behavior, beliefs and characteristics related by a common bond	
26. **Status**	Z. prejudice based on physical appearance	
27. **Stereotype**	AA. belief that race is the primary determinant of traits and capacities which produce superiority of a particular race and inferiority or dehumanization of others	
28. **Stigma**	BB. personal experiences, attractions, identification; genetic and gender-associated behaviors	
29. **Tolerance**	CC. impairments which hinder may hinder full participation in society	
30. **Xenophobia**	DD. attitude, prejudice, stereotyping or discrimination on the basis of gender	

Place the letter for the correct meaning in the box on the right, which corresponds to the word(s).

Diversity Definitions - Real Life Examples

WORDS	EXAMPLES
Acceptance	*My friend's family treats me like one of them, even though we are a different religion.*
Ageism	
Bigotry	
Body – Ideal Image	
Classism	
Culture	
Disability	
Discrimination	
Diversity	
Ethnic Group	
Ethnocentrism	
Equality	
Gender Bias	
Gender Identity	
Human Rights	
Inclusion	
Lookism	
Prejudice	
Race	
Racism	
Religion	
Sexism	
Sexual Orientation	
Social Subcultures	
Spirituality	
Status	
Stereotype	
Stigma	
Tolerance	
Xenophobia	

Diversity Definitions

FOR THE FACILITATOR

I. Purpose

To learn and personalize terminology as it is used in the context of this book.

II. General Comments

A common frame of reference helps teens understand the concepts related to diversity.

III. Possible Activities

a. Ask teens to share situations wherein people used words they didn't understand.
b. Explain that they will learn and personalize some terms related to diversity.
c. Distribute the *Diversity Definitions* handout, page 13.
d. Ask volunteers to take turns reading aloud the words and definitions.
e. Encourage teens to share personal experiences with each concept.
f. Advise teens to turn over their papers and not look at the definitions.
g. Distribute the *Meaning Match-Up* handout, page 14.
h. Divide teens into teams to complete the matching exercise jointly. Alternatively advise individuals to work independently.
i. Ask teams or individuals to share their responses.

Possibilities

1. H	5. U	9. X	13. B	17. Z	21. J	25. P	29. S
2. L	6. Y	10. A	14. T	18. K	22. DD	26. Q	30. V
3. I	7. CC	11. O	15. F	19. M	23. BB	27. R	
4. G	8. C	12. E	16. D	20. AA	24. N	28. W	

j. Distribute the *Real Life Examples* handout page 15.
k. Ask a volunteer to read aloud the example.

Game Option

- Divide teens into two teams.
- Teens may refer to their *Diversity Definitions* handout, page 13, for assistance.
- Each team completes the handout.
- Teams reconvene, ideally facing each other.
- Opposing team members take turns reading aloud examples in random order.
- The opposite team members guess which words were exemplified.

Individual Option

- Individuals complete the handout and then share their examples.

IV. Enrichment Activities

a. Encourage teens to share the most meaningful concept they learned in the session.
b. Role Plays
   - Ask teens to pair up and briefly practice role plays of the terms on the handout.
   - Teens re-convene and perform.
   - Audience guesses the term(s) portrayed.

Example:
A senior citizen requests an application to work at a fast food restaurant.
The manager says, "We're not hiring."
After the person leaves, manager says to another worker "That person is too old to work in fast food."
Audience might guess that these terms apply: ageism, bigotry, discrimination, prejudice, stereotype, etc.

Diversity Dances

Routines I

You're one of us . . . . (point to audience and self)
And that's a plus . . . . (make a plus sign in the air)
We never measure . . . . (pretend to use a ruler)
Your rank or treasure . . . . . (pretend to pull out money out of your pocket)
Acceptance and inclusion . . (show with arms in a hugging position)
Are no illusion . . . . (pretend to look through binoculars)
We care for each other . . . . (point to self and audience)
Like sister and brother . . . . (hand motion to show a shorter and taller child)

ACCEPTANCE, INCLUSION

Wealth and money . . . . (rub middle finger and thumb together)
Can be funny . . . . (point to the sides of your upturned lips)
Some go to all ends . . . . . . (point to both sides of the room)
To buy their friends . . . . (pretend to pay money from your palm)
Those without . . . . (palms up)
Need not pout . . . . (point to the sides of your downturned lips)
The tables may turn . . . . . . (turn around a few times)
And they may earn . . . . (point to an upturned palm)
Things far above . . . . (point upward)
Like respect and love . . . . . (point to your heart)

CLASSISM

How you look . . . . (pretend to look in a hand mirror)
Is just a hook . . . . (form the shape of a hook with your hand)
To snare unaware . . . . (motion like pulling in a fish)
With a face that is fair . . . . . (point to your face)
The way you look . . . . (point to your body)
Like cover on book . . . . (put palms together like closing a book)
Shows not what's inside . . . (open palms)
But you cannot hide . . . . . . (put hands in front of your face)
That you care and share . . . (point to heart)
And are willing to bear . . . . (bend forward)
My burdens and dreams . . . (point to your back and your head)
And on you I may lean . . . . (lean to the side)

LOOKISM

Like a label . . . . (point to your forehead)
Is to be unable . . . . (shrug)
Pointed at, blamed . . . . (point at audience)
Called ugly names . . . . (surround your mouth with hands like a megaphone)
Yet in the end . . . . (pretend to point to the bottom item on a list)
We will transcend . . . . (hands floating upward)
Our strength and talent . . . . (pretend to play a musical instrument)
Will make us valiant . . . . . . (both thumbs up)

STIGMA

Diversity Dances

Routines II

If they're young and wear hoodies . . . . (pull up an imaginary hoodie)
They're after your goodies . . . . (pretend to grab something)
Like birds of a feather . . . . (make flying motions with arms)
They hang out together . . . . (put index and middle fingers together to show closeness)
They love drugs . . . . (give self a shot in the arm)
They are thugs . . . . (punch the air)

STEREOTYPE

Different hue . . . . (point to skin on arm)
Different view . . . . (look through imaginary binoculars)
Our accents seem strange . . . . (cup your ear as trying to hear)
And yet we remain . . . . (point to audience and self)
Respected . . . . (bow)
Connected . . . . (clasp hands together)
Individual people . . . . (point to each other)
Unlike yet equal . . . . (palms up as if weighing two items the same weight)

TOLERANCE

Push them back . . . . (point thumbs backward)
Push them back . . . . (point thumbs backward)
Way back . . . . (point thumbs further back)
Keep them down . . . . (push hands down)
Keep them down . . . . (push hands down)
Low down . . . . (push hands further down)
We don't care . . . . (shrug shoulders)
We don't care . . . . (shrug shoulders)
How they fare . . . . (shrug shoulders)
We're the best . . . . (point your nose in air)
We're the best . . . . (point your nose in air)
Trash the rest . . . . (pretend to throw something at audience)

DISCRIMINATION, PREJUDICE

Write your own lyrics and dance routines.

Diversity Dances

What Do You Stand For?

Circle *True* or *False* then give an example from your life.

1. True False I easily accept people who are different from me.

Example: ____________________

2. True False I enjoy hearing stories told by elderly people.

Example: ____________________

3. True False I have friends whose race is different from mine.

Example: ____________________

4. True False I have friends from different nationalities.

Example ____________________

5. True False I have friends whose religious beliefs differ from mine.

Example ____________________

6. True False I do not judge people based on looks, economic status, sports ability, color, etc.

Example ____________________

7. True False I do not choose friends based on their finances.

Example ____________________

8. True False I am aware of individual differences among members of the same group.

Example ____________________

9. True False I respect people's views even if I do not agree.

Example ____________________

10. True False I believe in equal rights for all.

Example ____________________

Diversity Dances

FOR THE FACILITATOR

I. Purpose

To use concepts related to diversity and discrimination in a meaningful way.

II. General Comments

Definitions come to life as teens compose lyrics and choreograph routines.

III. Possible Activities

a. Before session photocopy enough *Diversity Definitions* handouts, page 13 for all participants.
b. Make two or three copies of *Diversity Dances and Routines I and II*, pages 17 and 18.
c. Cut on the broken lines; the duplicate cutouts will be given to teammates later.
d. Photocopy enough *What Do You Stand For?* handouts, page 19 for all participants.
e. When session begins, ask a few volunteers to demonstrate their favorite sports cheers.
f. Explain that teens will write lyrics and choreograph routines related to discrimination and diversity.
g. Distribute the *Diversity Definitions* handout and review the terms.
h. Divide teens into teams of two or three members.
i. Position teams as far apart as possible to allow space to practice lyrics and routines.
j. Give each team a different set of cut-outs from *Diversity Dances Routines I and II*, pages 17 and 18; one team will have copies Acceptance and Inclusion, another will have Classism, etc.
k. Allow a few minutes for teams to practice the lyrics and routines.
l. The group re-convenes; teams take turns reading lyrics and performing routines.
m. Audience guesses the concepts portrayed (possible answers are parenthesized on cut-outs).
n. Encourage teens to discuss whether the dance showed a helpful or hurtful concept and why.
o. Divide teens into teams again with two or three members; teens will compose their own routines.
p. Teams decide which concept to portray from the *Diversity Definitions*, list page _____.
q. Team members brainstorm dances and write the lyrics and routines on the backs of their cutouts or they may use the box at the bottom of page 18, W*rite Your Own Lyrics and Dance Routines.*
r. Allow time for practice.
s. The group re-convenes; teams take turns performing lyrics and dances.
t. Audience guesses the concepts portrayed.
u. Ask performers why they chose the particular concept portrayed.
v. Ask the audience to describe the feelings they experienced while watching the dances.
w. Encourage a discussion of any terms that were not addressed in the routines.
x. Ask volunteers to share their life experiences with the diversity-related concepts.

IV. Enrichment Activities

a. Distribute the W*hat Do You Stand For?* handout, page 19 and allow time for completion.
b. Facilitator or volunteer reads the statements aloud.
c. Ask teens to stand up for all statements for which they answered True.
d. Encourage teens to share their examples.
e. Ask teens who did **not** stand up for all statements which attitudes and actions they want to adopt.
f. Encourage teens who **did** stand up or those specific statements to share ways to embrace diversity.
g. Encourage teens to discuss what they learned about themselves and others by doing this exercise.
h. Share the following words of Martin Niemoller, a protestant pastor and foe of Hitler who was put in concentration camps:
First they came for the Communists, and I did not speak out – because I was not a Communist.
Then they came for the Socialists, and I did not speak out – because I was not a Socialist.
Then they came for the trade unionists, and I did not speak out – because I was not a trade unionist.
Then they came for the Jews, and I did not speak out – because I was not a Jew.
Then they came for me, and there was no one left to speak out for me.
i. Ask teens what the story means to them today.

My Many Cultures

CULTURE	BELIEFS	EXPECTED ACTIONS	OUTCOMES
Parents and/or Caregivers			
Extended family, grandparents, etc.			
Friends			
School			
Work/Volunteer			
Ethnicity and/or race			
Music			
Fashion			
Religion			
Social groups			
Teenage culture			
Romance			
Inclusion vs. Exclusion			
Social Media			
Other			

My Many Cultures

FOR THE FACILITATOR

I. Purpose

To identify the many cultures to which teens belong.

II. General Comments

Teens consider their groups' attitudes, norms and values that may have positive or negative effects.

III. Possible Activities

a. Write on the board: **Culture = similar behavior, beliefs and characteristics of a particular group of people and may relate to age, body, disability, ethnicity, family, gender, neighborhood, race, religion, sexual orientation, social, spiritual, status or other common bonds.**

b. Ask teens to brainstorm the many cultures to which they belong.

c. Distribute the *My Many Cultures* handout and ask teens to brainstorm a few examples.

d. Explain that teens may belong to cultures that promote helpful or hurtful beliefs and actions.

e. Encourage objectivity and honesty as they consider their cultural influences.

f. Allow time for completion; then encourage teens to share their responses.

Possibilities below include positive aspects (+) *and negative aspects* (-) *of various cultures:*

Culture	Beliefs	Expected Actions	Outcomes
Parents and/or Caregivers	(+) #1 person - education is 1st. (+) #2 person - responsibility is 1st. (-) Drugs are okay.	(+) Do homework first. (+) Work part-time job. (-) Use substances and drugs	(+) Earn a college degree. (+) Pay own expenses. (-) Become addicted.
Extended family, grandparents, etc.	(+) Family unity is #1. (-) Family feuds are fine.	(+) Spend time together. (-) Take sides.	(+) Have a support system. (-) Continue the battles.
Friends	(+) Loyalty is major. (-) Friends are disloyal,	(+) Defend each other. (-) Gossip.	(+) Stay connected. (-) Breakup friendships.
School	(+) Knowledge is power, (-) School is worthless,	(+) Do my best. (-) Cut class.	(+) Earn my diploma. (-) Drop out.
Work/Volunteer	(+) The customer is #1. (-) Money matters most.	(+) Provide great service. (-) Give little, take much.	(+) Increase sales. (-) Lose business.
Ethnicity and/or race	(+) My roots have value. (-) My heritage holds me back.	(+) Learn about ancestors. (-) Ignore valuable facts.	(+) Carry out traditions. (-) Deny a part of me.
Music	(+) Rock, rap, or ________ reigns. (-) Hate other music.	(+) Enjoy CDs and concerts. (-) Trash other types.	(+) Learn the lyrics. (-) Miss out on music.
Fashion	(+) Goth, punk, or ________ is best. (-) Other styles are ugly.	(+) Wear the clothes. (-) Mock different tastes.	(+) Represent a style. (-) Be narrow-minded.
Religion	(+) My religion is my truth. (-) Others have no value.	(+) Attend services, read the sacred books, pray. (-) Put down others' views.	(+) Stick to my beliefs, give time, effort and funds. (-) Disrespect difference.
Social groups	(+) My clubs, band, sports, etc. are worthwhile. (-) Exclusive cliques rule.	(+) Attend meetings; work together, practice. (-) Don't accept outsiders.	(+) Make friends with like-minded people. (-) Fear being outcast.
Teenage culture	(+) Teens have promise. (-) Fights are mighty.	(+) Pursue goals with zeal. (-) Go to war against rivals.	(+) Reach full potential. (-) Endanger self & others.
Romance	(+) A partner is a plus. (-) No partner = I'm a loser	(+) Find positive people. (-) Pair up with anyone	(+) Have a healthy bond. (-) Be miserable and/or deny my values.
Inclusion vs Exclusion	(+) Variety spices life. (-) Differences aren't okay.	(+) Welcome new people. (-) Stick to the same old.	(+) Expand circle of friends. (-) Stagnate socially.
Social Media	(+) Consider privacy and people's feelings. (-) Be outrageous to gain followers.	(+) Think before sharing. (-) Tell all about self and others.	(+) Safeguard self and others. (-) Endanger self and others.

IV. Enrichment Activities

Encourage a discussion about the pros and cons of protest group cultures *(example–animal rights proponents that carry signs about cruelty at circuses).*

Melting Pot, Salad or Stew?

In a melting pot, ingredients lose their colors, shapes and tastes to become a puree.
In a salad, foods keep their colors, shapes and tastes.
In a stew, items mingle to form broth but keep their colors, shapes and tastes.

Theories about Immigration

Melting Pot	Salad Bowl	Cultural Stew

In a *Melting Pot* newcomers often give up ethnic traditions to fit into the new country's culture.	In a *Salad Bowl* people from different cultures are welcomed as valuable contributors to the whole.	In a *Cultural Stew* people are encouraged to blend in and yet have distinction.
____________	____________	____________

Put each statement's letter in the line at the bottom of the box that best describes it.

a. It's better to blend in than to stand out.
b. Go with the flow on small stuff but stick to your beliefs when it matters.
c. Out with the old and in with the new.
d. Unique is interesting.
e. Different is weird.
f. Be totally you in every situation.
g. Keep the best of both worlds.
h. Obey the new country's laws but wear ethnic clothes.

Fold and tear on the dotted line then write your responses anonymously.

All people want to be accepted.

1. What have you given up or hidden in order to blend in? ____________________
2. What part of your individuality would you never want to lose? ____________________
3. Share a time you showed your true self and how people reacted. ____________________
4. Are you in a melting pot, salad bowl or stew? ____________________
   Explain: ____________________

Melting Pot, Salad or Stew?

FOR THE FACILITATOR

I. Purpose

To consider the older melting pot theory, the newer salad bowl concept, and the cultural stew which is the best of both worlds.

II. General Comments

Theories about immigration relate to teens from racial, ethnic and other minorities but can extend to anyone who wants acceptance in a culture.

- The *Melting Pot* became a phrase for people of different cultures coming to this world. It promotes assimilation and expects minorities to give up their uniqueness to blend in with the majority.
- The *Salad Bowl* promotes multiculturalism which celebrates differences and encourages minorities to maintain and take pride and joy in their identities.
- The *Cultural Stew* suggests compromise: blend in when it benefits both newcomer and majority and/or on insignificant issues; retain and respect important traditions and values.

III. Possible Activities

a. Distribute the *Melting Pot, Salad or Stew?* handout.

b. Ask for a show of hands regarding preferences for pureed food as in a melting pot or chewy, fresh, crunchy food as in a salad bowl or stew (most prefer chewy vs. baby food).

c. Ask a volunteer to read the introduction and explanations in the boxes aloud.

d. Allow time for completion.

e. Encourage teens to share their responses for a-g.

Possibilities:

Melting Pot	Salad Bowl	Cultural Stew
a, c, e	d, f	b, g, h

f. Ask a volunteer to collect the responses for Numbers 1-4 (torn from the bottom of the page).

g. Ask a volunteer to read the responses aloud and to elicit feedback.

h. Pose the following questions and encourage discussion and debate:

- How would you describe this school or facility: a melting pot? salad? or stew?
- Would you like to see it better blended or with more variety? Explain.
- In what ways does the peer culture expect people to look and act a certain way to be popular?
- How can you celebrate your own uniqueness? (show it, tell about your background).
- How can you demonstrate that you value people's differences? (ask questions, listen, show you care).
- When people go to a new place, what do they do to try to blend in? (talk, act, dress the same).
- What traits in a newcomer make it hard to gain acceptance? (a difference or self-consciousness).
- What attitudes among peers make it hard for an outsider to blend in? (fear of the unknown).

IV. Enrichment Activities

Encourage teens to discuss and debate which they think is best: melting pot, salad bowl or cultural stew, and to explain their reasons.

The ♥ of Diversity

In each human heart is a tiger, a pig, a donkey and a bird. Diversity of character is due to their unequal activity.

~ adapted from a quote by **Ambrose Bierce**

Tiger

Traits
Example: powerful

Tigers are known for their fiery passion.
How can you stand-up for diversity?

Pig

Traits
Example: intelligent

Pigs are so intelligent that they help each other escape from well-built fences.
How can you help free penned-in people?

Donkey

Traits
Example: loyal

Donkeys are beasts of burden.
How can you lighten an underdog's load?

Bird

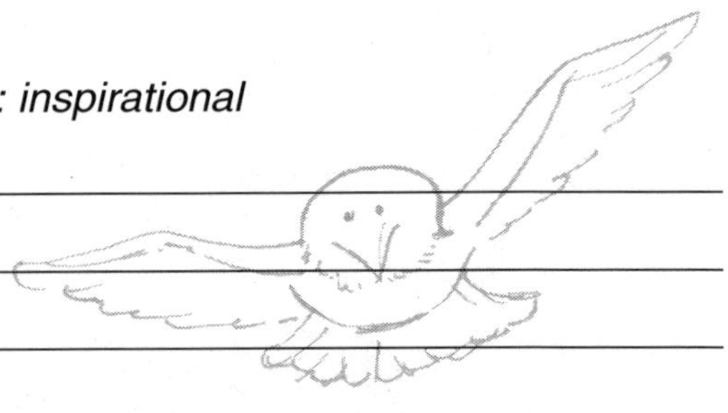

Traits
Example: inspirational

A bird's song is one of the most beautiful sounds. How can your voice awaken a spirit of acceptance?

The ♥ of Diversity

FOR THE FACILITATOR

I. **Purpose**

To recognize symbolic animal traits which are also found in most people in varying amounts.

II. **General Comments**

Teens are helped to focus on common bonds and develop acceptance and empathy.

III. **Possible Activities**

a. Before session ask a volunteer to draw a heart with an animal in each chamber (tiger, pig, donkey, bird).

b. Write the quote that was adapted from Ambrose Bierce (from the handout) on the board and ask for interpretations (the same traits in assorted activities or amounts create individual differences).

c. Distribute *The ♥ of Diversity* handout; ask volunteers to read aloud the examples and questions.

d. Explain that the examples are positive but teens may list positive and negative traits for each animal.

Team Option

- Divide teens into four teams (one for each animal); a writer for each team lists its animal's characteristics and brainstorms responses to the question.
- Teens re-convene and the writers share their teams' ideas.

Individual Option

- Teens record their own responses then share their ideas.

Possible Responses

- **Tiger Traits**: courageous, free-spirited, yet can be territorial and aggressive. Teens can stand-up for diversity by making friends with different kinds of peers, learning about racial, ethnic and social groups and appreciating music, dance, art, sports, literature and drama that celebrate cultures and/or lifestyles. They can promote school policies and legislation for inclusion.
- **Pig Traits:** sociable, independent, highly trainable, yet they are associated with greed. Teens can free *penned-in* outsiders by promoting anti-bullying campaigns, inviting peers with differences into clubs and activities, and reaching out through technology (send friendly texts, connect on social media sites, etc.).
- **Donkey Traits:** adaptable, focused on self-preservation (they refuse dangerous commands), diligent, yet often appear stubborn. Teens can lighten an underdog's load by befriending, helping and advocating for the person or group. They may ask open-ended questions, reflect feelings and help people to problem solve.
- **Bird Traits:** motivational, peaceful (dove), wise (owl), able to overcome (gravity), yet there are birds of prey that devour others. Teens can *voice* a spirit of acceptance through their spoken and written words and actions. They can journal, write articles for the school paper, letters to their local newspapers, lyrics and music; their pictures can be worth a thousand words as they make posters or photograph situations.
- **Other Traits** that may live in every heart are infinite but teens may note love, compassion, joy, honesty, self-sacrifice (as well as sadness, anger, selfishness, loneliness, etc.).

e. Encourage a debate between teens who agree and disagree with the adapted Bierce quote. They may agree that people use their traits differently and positives or negatives may seem to dominate. They may disagree with the idea that humans harbor animal characteristics.

IV. **Enrichment Activities**

a. Ask teams or individuals to substitute different animals in the quote – *In each heart there are a _____, _____, _____, and a _____.*

b. Ask teens to describe the traits their selected animals represent.

c. Ask teens *"What other traits do you believe live in every human heart?"*

How Culture Affects Me and Others

Select an issue to write about on the back of this page.
You do not need to reveal it to anyone.

LIST OF TOPICS

Describe the dynamics between you and others in your household. Include the emotional closeness or distance among you and issues about which you agree and disagree.

Describe racial, ethnic and cultural influences on your appearance, clothing, thought process, etc. Include the importance or insignificance of these to you and people who are close to you.

Discuss your attitudes toward food, your holiday favorite foods and forbidden foods (for religious, cultural or other reasons). Include ways, and whether or not, you stick to the rules.

Discuss your needs for privacy. Include your comfort or discomfort about sharing personal information with educational or health care professionals or other people.

Discuss peers' tolerance and acceptance of **your family's culture** and traditions.

Discuss your views of time and if or how you learned the importance of being on time. Share experiences you have had with people who view time differently.

Discuss your level of comfort with casual touching like hugging acquaintances. Include your needs regarding personal space and crowds.

Discuss the role of your culture in shaping your spiritual beliefs and practices.

Discuss if your culture influences expressing or hiding emotions. Explain how this has affected you.

Discuss society and media's view of your body (shape, size, and/or weight).

Discuss your tolerance and acceptance toward **peers of a culture different** from yours.

Discuss peers' tolerance and acceptance of **your culture.**

Discuss your culture's expectations about dating and marriage and its impact on you.

Discuss your music and dance preferences and how they are influenced by your culture.

Discuss your tolerance and acceptance of **peers' families' culture** and traditions.

Discuss your sports involvement and how it is influenced by race, ethnicity and/or values.

How Culture Affects Me and Others

FOR THE FACILITATOR

Purpose

To recognize the role culture plays in thoughts, feelings, interpersonal relations, interests, etc.

General Comments

Teens journal about a private issue they prefer not to share with the group to develop insight and avoid monitoring their words to prevent offending someone. Teens talk about another topic during peer interviews and understand that their ideas may be disclosed to the group.

Possible Activities

a. Write on the board *Favorites.*
b. Ask teens to share their favorites (song, movie, etc.) as a volunteer lists them on the board.
c. Ask how teens developed their preferences (possibly friends and family influenced them).
d. Write on the board *Culture* and ask its meaning (similar behavior, beliefs and characteristics of a particular group of people and may relate to age, disability, ethnicity, family, gender, race, religion, sexual orientation, social, spiritual, status or other common bond).
e. Ask about unconscious, automatic and unspoken rules teens live by at home and with friends.
f. List a few on the board to illustrate that within specific groups different expectations apply. Example – Family: *What happens in family stays in family.*
g. Distribute the *How Culture Affects Me and Others* handout.
h. Ask teens to take turns reading aloud the directions and the list of topics.
i. Ask teens to brainstorm additional relevant topics and list them on the board.
j Explain that teens may select topics from the board and/or from their handouts.
k. Ask teens to write about a topic they consider private; explain this will not be shared.
l. After they write their responses, teens partner with a peer.
m. Each teen selects a different topic to talk about when interviewed.
n. Partners interview each other and document their partner's responses on notebook paper.
o. After the interviews, each pair sits at the front of the room and share each others' responses.
p. Teens may decline to have their responses shared with the group.
q. Ask teens to identify an aspect about themselves that they now know has cultural origins.
r. Ask teens to state at least one concept they learned about another culture.
s. Some teens may find the activity intense and may need to debrief as a group or individually; encourage participants to share feelings that surfaced during the session.

Enrichment Activities

a. Discuss the importance of telling educational and health care professionals about their beliefs and values regarding privacy, family, spirituality and other issues.
b. Ask teens if they receive conflicting messages from home and the community and how they handle the discrepancy; elicit suggestions from peers.

The King and the Pawn

> ***After the game the king and the pawn go into the same box.***
> **~ Italian Proverb**

On the chessboard the king is prized, the pawn is comparatively powerless.
What happens when they enter the chess box?

____

____

____

Imagine your own endings to these sentence starters:

After the ball game the *star* and the *player who sat on the sideline* ______________________

____

After the dance the *life of the party* and the *wallflower* ______________________

____

After class the *A student* and the *C student* ______________________

____

After graduation the *most popular person* and the *person who was usually ignored* ____________

____

After the concert the *lead singer* and the *back-up singer* ______________________

____

After the tennis match, the *winner* and the *loser* ______________________

____

Feel free to add other sentence starters and completions below.

After ____

____

After ____

____

After ____

____

The King and the Pawn

FOR THE FACILITATOR

I. Purpose

To illustrate that differences which seem to separate teens are fleeting and contingent on the setting.

II. General Comments

Awareness of commonalities helps decrease divisiveness, comparisons and competition.

III. Possible Activities

a. If possible bring a chess set or a picture of a chess set, with the chess pieces in a box.
b. Ask a volunteer to explain the relative value of a king and a pawn (highest and lowest).
c. Ask teens when and where the values matter (during the game and on the chessboard).
d. Ask teens what happens after the game (pieces and the board are put away in a box together).
e. Ask teens what the king, pawn and other parts of the game become in the box (pieces whose values only matter on the chessboard).
f. Ask teens how the chess analogy applies to people (in certain settings some seem to have higher value but away from those arenas they may be equals or roles may be reversed).
g. Distribute *The King and the Pawn* handout and ask a volunteer to read aloud the Italian proverb.
h. Allow time for completion.
i. Encourage teens to share their responses.

Possibilities

- The *star* and the *person on the sidelines* go into the locker room where they are both athletes, members of the same team, possibly good friends, etc.
- The *life of the party* and the *wallflower* go home where they are both people with hopes, challenges, goals, etc.
- The *A student* and the *C student* go to another class where their grades may be reversed and where they are both learners doing their best to gain knowledge.
- The *most popular* and the *person who is usually ignored* go into the real world where they both pursue their dreams.
- The *lead singer* and the *back-up singer* go backstage where they are both vocalists with a passion for music.
- The *winner* and the *loser*, who know their roles could reverse, practice to hone their skills for the next tennis match.

j. Encourage a discussion about whether grades or popularity in high school predict future success. Many average students have created multi-million dollar empires and unpopular kids have become huge celebrities.

Enrichment Activities

Ask teens to consider commonalities amidst diversity using *"At the end of the day…"*

Examples

- At the end of the day, regardless of race or ethnicity - people love their families, care about careers, want the best for their kids, enjoy their special foods and festivals, etc.
- At the end of the day, regardless of religion - people seek truth, strength and comfort in something greater than themselves.
- At the end of the day, regardless of finances - people value their belongings, want salary raises and want to maintain or upgrade their standard of living.
- At the end of the day, regardless of disabilities, people want to use their abilities to the max.

On Second Thought . . .

For each situation, jot down your first thought which will remain private. Then write your second thought, which you may wish to share.

Situation	First Thought (Close-Minded)	Second Thought (Open-Minded)
Ex: I see a cashier with gray hair.	*That line will be slow.*	*That cashier is experienced.*
My overweight friend wants to be in the fashion show.		
My classmate in a wheelchair wants to play basketball.		
My assistant principal is from an ethnic group I have heard bad things about.		
My family distrusts anyone in a culture different from ours.		
A male at my school wants to be a professional ballet dancer.		
I need an organ transplant; the donor is of a race I don't trust.		
My single parent marries someone of a different race.		
My sibling is engaged to someone whose religion is different from ours.		
My friend reveals a same sex attraction.		
I want to be friends with someone from a different clique.		
My step-parent will not attend our religious institution.		
I want to date someone from a different socioeconomic group.		
A person I know wants to be the opposite gender.		
A friend at my school is pregnant.		
Other		
Other		

On Second Thought . . .

FOR THE FACILITATOR

I. Purpose

To recognize that initial reactions may be prejudiced, but people can re-think and embrace diversity.

II. General Comments

Teens consider whether culture matters in life and death situations as well as in other circumstances.

III. Possible Activities

a. Before session recruit three volunteers to play victim, rescuer and onlooker.
b. Allow time for practice before they perform this mock video:
   Victim lies on the floor.
   Rescuer kneels next to victim, yells *Call 911, no pulse, no breathing.* Onlooker dials 911.
   Rescuer, **without any real physical contact**, pretends to start mouth to mouth breathing.
   Onlooker says, *"Stop, you're from a different race!"*
c. Ask teens *"What was ridiculous about the video?"* (that race would matter in saving a life).
d. Tell teens they will examine their first thoughts which may be closed-minded then reconsider.
e. Distribute the *On Second Thought…* handout.
f. A volunteer reads the directions and example aloud; allow time for completion.

Encourage teens to share their open-minded second thoughts.

Possibilities

Situation	First Thought (Close-Minded)	Second Thought Open-Minded)
I see a cashier with gray hair.	*That line will be slow.*	*That cashier is experienced.*
My overweight friend wants to be in the fashion show.	*The clothes won't look good on you.*	*You can be trendy.*
My classmate in a wheelchair wants to play basketball.	*No way.*	*Wheelchair basketball is popular.*
My assistant principal is from an ethnic group I have heard bad things about.	*I will have a difficult time showing respect.*	*This assistant principal may contribute to my education.*
My family distrusts anyone in a culture different from ours.	*I agree with them.*	*Outsiders may become friends.*
A male at my school wants to be a professional ballet dancer.	*How feminine!*	*Both male and female ballet dancers are valued.*
I need an organ transplant; the donor is of a race I don't trust.	*Is there a donor from my own race?*	*Race doesn't matter; this person may save my life.*
My single parent marries someone of a different race.	*I don't want a step-parent from that race.*	*Love is about the heart not the heritage.*
My sibling is engaged to someone of a different religion from ours.	*How will they raise their kids?*	*Their children will be exposed to both religions.*
My friend reveals a same sex attraction.	*People will think I'm that way.*	*I support my friend's courage.*
I want to be friends with someone from a different clique.	*My friends won't approve.*	*I make my own choices.*
My step-parent will not attend our religious institution.	*This person is disrupting our family's beliefs.*	*I respect my step-parent's right to individual beliefs.*
I want to date someone from a different socioeconomic group.	*I can't. Money matters.*	*I can. Feelings matter.*
A person I know wants to be the opposite gender.	*That's weird!*	*I hope the person will have a better life by being true to self.*
A friend at my school is pregnant.	*I would never let that happen to me.*	*I'm going to stand by my friend.*

IV. Enrichment Activities

Encourage teens to share recent situations where they could have been more open-minded.

PHYSICAL DIVERSITY 2

Sometimes people are beautiful.
Not in looks. Not in what they say. Just in what they are.
~ Markus Zusak

Lookism from Head to Toe

Lookism is prejudice based on physical appearance, especially if the physical appearance is different from society's standards.

It can also mean preferential treatment given to physically attractive people.

A caricature is a cartoon, drawing or description of somebody's characteristics; comical or grotesque, not meant to be unkind.

Draw and/or describe *overstated* features that show *supposed* teen standards of attractiveness.

Features	Female	Male
Hair		
Eyes		
Nose		
Mouth		
Chest		
Arms and hands		
Waist		
Hips		
Butt		
Legs		
Feet		
Add fashion, piercings, tattoos and/or other trends		

What does *lookism* overlook? ____________________

____

Lookism from Head to Toe

FOR THE FACILITATOR

I. Purpose

To foster awareness of the unrealistic standards of attractiveness and the stereotypes of femininity and masculinity promoted in the media and society.

II. General Comments

Teens consider the sources and challenge pop culture's dictates about beauty, body (shape, size and weight), and machoism.

III. Possible Activities

a. Although the *Lookism from Head to Toe* handout provides space for caricatures, large chart paper or butcher paper and colored markers are recommended. Option: clay for teens to sculpt.
b. Write *Lookism* and *Caricature* on the board and elicit definitions similar to those on the handout.
c. Tell teens they will be drawing. You set boundaries: no genitals (be aware that female breasts and butts for both sexes will be depicted unless you request they are not included). If you prefer, separate the males and females for this session.
d. Distribute the *Lookism from Head to Toe* handout and ask volunteers to read the items in the first column.

Team Option

- If both sexes are participating, divide into male and female teams; teams depict their own genders.
- Give each team large paper and markers and allow time for all teammates to add to the drawings.
- Teens re-convene and share their artwork with the group.

Individual Option

- Allow time for teens to draw their own genders on large paper or on the handout.
- Encourage teens to share their work with the group.

Both Options: Ask *What does Lookism overlook?* (inner traits – compassion, talents, etc.) and remind the group that *beauty is in the eye of the beholder.*

Both Options: Ask the following questions - concepts to elicit are parenthesized:

1. Who sets society's standards for attractiveness? (people and the media in each culture).
2. How realistic are the standards? (unrealistic for the majority of people).
3. Are standards the same throughout the world? (no, they vary greatly).
4. Who spreads the word? (magazines, music videos, movies, TV, websites, advertisements, etc.).
5. Who benefits? (advertisers who promise people they'll look better, be successful, have closer relationships, etc. if people use their products; movie and video producers, magazine publishers).
6. Who suffers? (real people who compare themselves to touched-up photos or pop culture idols).
7. What happens when we receive the same messages from a variety of sources? (we believe them).
8. What's the problem with set standards for femininity and masculinity? (they dictate false ideals, do not allow for individual differences and they stereotype the genders).
9. Introduce *halo effect* whereby attractive people are presumed to have other positive qualities like better personalities. Ask teens if one's appearance shows a true picture of his/her performance in the classroom, the community, etc.

IV. Enrichment Activities

a. Write *Good looks can be …* on the board and ask teens to brainstorm opposites that apply (tall or short, slim or curvy, muscular or lean, light or dark, etc.)
b. Ask what teens can do to promote diversity regarding appearance? (research other cultures' ideas of attractiveness; play up their own individuality).
c. Encourage a discussion about health at any size; elicit that there are over/underweight people who eat nutritious foods and exercise; address heredity's influence on body build.

Smart Sensitivity

1. Tape a sign that says *Wheelchair* on a chair.
   Actor #1 sits in the wheelchair.
   Actor #2 walks up to the person and starts a friendly conversation while standing.
   Narrator asks audience,
   What's wrong with this?

2. **Actor** calls someone on cell phone and says,
   I was just talking with the disabled student.
   Narrator asks audience,
   What's wrong with this?

3. **Actor #1** walks up to **Actor #2** and offers
   Please have a piece of my candy.
   Actor #2 says *No thanks.*
   Actor #1 asks *Why?*
   Narrator asks audience,
   What's wrong with this?

4. **Actor #1** asks *What do you want to eat?*
   Actor #2 stutters *Ch, ch, ch …*
   Actor #1 says *Cheese.*
   Actor #2 shakes head *No.*
   Actor #1 says *Chips.*
   Actor #2 shakes head *No.*
   Narrator asks audience,
   What's wrong with this?

5. **Actor #1** puts tongue on roof of mouth and mumbles,
   Can I borrow twenty bucks?
   Actor #2 nods head.
   Actor #1 holds out a hand for the money.
   Actor #2 asks,
   Why are you holding out your hand?
   Narrator asks audience,
   What happened?

6. **Actor #1** sits with eyes closed (the person has a visual impairment).
   Actor #2 walks up and asks,
   Do you want to go to a movie with me?
   Narrator asks audience,
   What's wrong with this?

7. Tape a sign that says *Wheelchair* on a chair,
   Actor #1 sits in the wheelchair.
   Actor #2 walks up, sits opposite the person, and very slowly and loudly asks,
   How are you doing?
   Narrator asks audience,
   What's wrong with this?

8. **Actor #1** cups one ear with one hand (the person has a hearing impairment)
   Actor #2 faces away from the person and asks,
   Do you want to go to the game?
   Narrator asks audience,
   What's wrong with this?

Smart Sensitivity

FOR THE FACILITATOR

I. Purpose

To be sensitive to people's needs without excessive emphasis on impairments.

II. General Comments

Teens learn how to increase people's comfort levels and to avoid labels and stereotypes.

III. Possible Activities

a. Before session make three photocopies of the *Smart Sensitivity* handout and cut on the broken lines.
b. Place each set of three in a stack; these will be scripts for mock videos (1-2 actors and narrator).
c. Before session ask teens with physical disabilities if they would be willing to share in group.
d. When session starts ask if anyone has had a broken arm, leg or had another injury.
e. Encourage teens to share how they felt and how their activities were affected.
f. Ask willing teens with physical impairments about their feelings and how activities are affected.
g. Ask previously injured teens and those with physical impairments if they categorize themselves as one of *the injured* or *the disabled* or as people who had or happen to have a physical impairment.
h. Emphasize that an impairment is a feature like eye color but it does not define a person's identity.
i. Explain that teens will perform short mock videos with one to two actors and a narrator.
j. Teens take turns picking up one of the stacks of scripts, deciding their roles and performing.
k. The audience shares their ideas regarding what is wrong and why.
   Possibilities corresponding to the numbers on the cut-outs:
   1. Towering above a person may cause discomfort; sit and talk at eye level.
   2. The phrase *Disabled student* suggests the impairment defines the person; don't label people, use the person's name.
   3. Asking *Why* pushes for disclosure of personal info (e.g., a medical issue).
   4. Finishing a sentence for a person who stutters is not helpful; wait and listen.
   5. Pretending to understand a person's speech causes mix-ups; admit you don't understand, ask the person to repeat what was said or to write the message.
   6. The person did not identify him/herself; say *Hi, it's Tom. Do you want to go to the concert?*
   7. Talking loudly to a person in a wheelchair assumes a hearing impairment; talk normally.
   8. Facing away makes it difficult to hear and lip read; face the person when speaking.
l. Write *HIV/AIDS* on the board and ask their meanings (HIV is a virus which destroys the immune system; people with AIDS cannot fight infections).
   - Ask teens how some people react to people with HIV/AIDS (avoidance).
   - Ask what it suggests about the avoiders (fear; ignorance about how it is spread).
m. Encourage a discussion about people with disfiguring conditions or diseases who are excluded.
   - How would you feel? (rejected, depressed, lonely, scared, angry, etc.).
   - How would you want to be treated? (accepted, included, like everyone else).

IV. Enrichment Activities

Create sticker labels of labels we put on others: *Handicapped, Nerd, Jock, etc.*

- Place a sticker on each student's back without them knowing what they received.
- Ask the group to *over act out* negative actions these labels receive.
- Everyone must guess what label they have based on how they were treated.
- Then, follow up with discussion:
  How are labels encouraging of discrimination?
  How did it feel to be treated in such a way?
  How can you improve how you treat others?

Sense-Less Quiz

Listen and watch – your group leader will give you the first three answers.

People with disabilities have the right to:

1. ______________________________
2. ______________________________
3. ______________________________

The following questions have no right or wrong answers.

4. How could you stay involved with your favorite sport or physical activity if you could not walk?

____
____
____

5. How could you dance if you could not hear the beat?

____
____
____

6. How could you run a race if you could not see?

____
____
____

7. How could you play a guitar without hands?

____
____
____

8. How could you know the when the umpire calls balls, strikes and outs if you could not hear?

____
____
____

Sense-Less Quiz

FOR THE FACILITATOR

I. Purpose

To develop empathy and consider the needs and rights of persons with physical disabilities.

II. General Comments

Teens first experience sensory deficits which block their success in a simulated test.

III. Possible Activities

a. Distribute the *Sense-Less Quiz* handout and explain that teens will take a test.
b. Tell teens *"If you watch and listen carefully, I will give you all the answers."*
c. Teens do not realize they will be unable to read or hear the answers.
d. Read aloud the test statement below and follow the parenthesized instructions.
People with disabilities have the right to:
1. *The answer to #1 is* (say in an **inaudible** voice) *Identity.*
2. *The answer to #2 is* (write on the board **too small to be read**) *Independence.*
3. *The answer to #3 is* (mouth the words; make it **hard to lip read**) *Reasonable accommodation.*

e. If teens ask for repetition, re-write or repeat the answers in an equally undecipherable manner.
f. Ask teens how they felt when responding to the test (possibly frustrated or angry).
g. Discuss that people with vision or hearing losses may have similar feelings.
h. Write the answers large enough to be read on the board; elicit concepts and examples:
1. Identity – a set of unique characteristics not overshadowed by impairment.
2. Independence – freedom from reliance on or control by others.
3. Reasonable accommodation – an adjustment that makes a system fair for a person with a proven need.

i. Point out that equality and fairness are not always the same.

Example

One seat is vacant on the bus.
A passenger with two legs and a passenger with one leg want the seat.
Both have an equal right to sit.

Ask

What is fair? (For the amputee to have the seat).

j. Possible responses corresponding to the numbers on the quiz:
4. Almost all sports are adaptable – wheelchair basketball, power wheelchair soccer, hand cycling, table tennis, sled hockey, bowling, archery, billiards, swimming; also teaching, watching and coaching.
5. Watch people who clap to the beat; dance without the music component.
6. Run with a guide runner.
7. Strum guitar with left foot and make chords with right foot.
8. Watch hand signals which were invented by a baseball player with a hearing impairment.

IV. Enrichment Activities

a. Ask how teens with impairments could receive education and employment in their chosen careers. Elicit the importance for stating needs, perseverance, workplace adaptations and accessibility.
b. Ask teens to divide into teams according to interests and conduct internet searches for people with disabilities who have achieved success in various sports, the arts, journalism, science, medicine, etc.
c. Encourage teens to explore organizations that help people with disabilities by providing Braille, guide dogs, sign language interpreters, adaptive sports, and other services.

Outside the Hourglass

Think outside the hourglass.

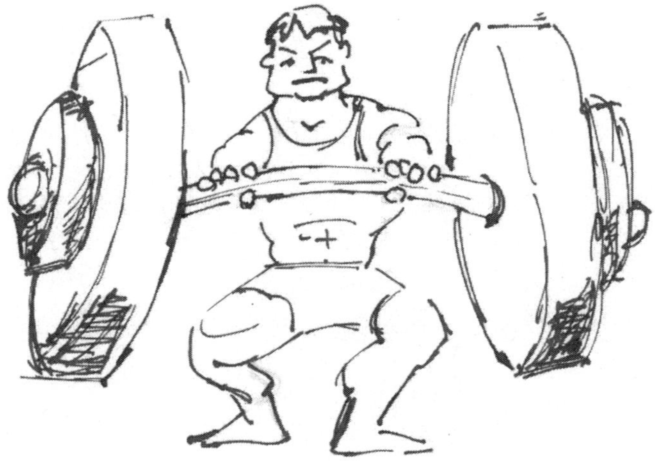

Beyond the barbell.

Looking glass lies.

Deeper than skin.

Outside the Hourglass

FOR THE FACILITATOR

I. Purpose

To create posters that refute media messages promoting a supposed standardized face and form.

II. General Comments

Teens analyze sample posters and then campaign for physical diversity. Use sensitivity if there is someone in the group with a physical difference.

III. Possible Activities

a. If possible, plan to provide large paper or butcher paper, pencils, colored markers, paints, etc.

b. Explain that teens will create posters about physical diversity.

c. Distribute the *Out of the Hourglass* handout; elicit teens' interpretations of the sample posters. Responses will vary.

Possibilities

- *Think outside the hourglass* – people may be trapped in the belief that the hourglass figure is ideal. To think *outside* means it's ok to be smaller, larger or shaped differently; there's more to people than their figures.
- *Beyond the barbell* – people may magnify the value of muscles. Character traits mean more than physical power: to fight (non-violently) for one's beliefs, to emotionally support friends in need.
- *Looking glass lies* – the media mirror dictates narrow parameters, and promises sex appeal and success for those who meet its standards. True value comes from within.
- *Deeper than skin* – face and form are superficial. The heart can care, love, understand, help people, change the world.

d. Distribute paper and art supplies if available; alternatively teens use the backs of their handouts.

e. Instruct individuals or teams to make posters that promote physical diversity.

f. Ideally, teens will be more creative if given less direction; encourage imagination.

g. If necessary suggest that they address diversity regarding the following:

- Size and shape
- Facial features
- Physical disabilities and abilities, and/or ways to adapt to visual or hearing impairments.

h. Teens may illustrate popular phrases e.g. attractiveness is *in the eye of the beholder*, a person can be like *a diamond in the rough,* it's important to be *comfortable in your own skin*, etc.

i. Encourage teens to show their posters and elaborate.

j. Encourage peers to provide additional interpretations.

k. Encourage teens to hang their posters on bulletin boards or other areas in the building.

IV. Enrichment Activities

Encourage teens to make mock commercials for fictitious products that promise diversity.

Examples

- A teen tells a friend, *Use this make-up and you won't look like a top model.*
- A salesperson tells a customer, *Buy this style because nobody wears it.*

Oppress or "UP-Press"?

List your team's twelve demanding ideas about body (shape, size and weight).
Then the opposing team will refute your statements.
Example: Everyone should have six-pack abs.

1. ______________________________

____

2. ______________________________

____

3. ______________________________

____

4. ______________________________

____

5. ______________________________

____

6. ______________________________

____

7. ______________________________

____

8. ______________________________

____

9. ______________________________

____

10. ______________________________

____

11. ______________________________

____

12. ______________________________

____

Oppress or "UP-Press"?

FOR THE FACILITATOR

I. Purpose

To identify and refute society's unrealistic standards for the *perfect body*.

II. General Comments

Media messages often cause unfair judgment of one's self and others leading to physical and emotional misery. In this game, teens brainstorm and dispute pop culture's fallacies.

III. Possible Activities

a. Before session photocopy two of the *Oppress or "UP-press"?* handouts.

b. Ask teens:
- *When thinking about society's standards, what body parts are supposed to be small?* (noses, waists, women's hands and feet).
- *Without reference to private parts, what parts of the body are supposed to be big?* (muscles, lips, chests).
- *What parts are supposed to be curvy?* (butts, women's hips).
- *What other media messages are promoted?* (perfect bodies are passports to success).

c. Write *Oppress* on the board and ask its meaning (to cruelly dominate; to be a source of stress).

d. Write *UP-press* on the board and ask *What could this made-up word mean?* (to press up or fight oppression).

e. Explain that each team will list twelve oppressing ideas about bodies promoted by pop-culture.

f. Divide the group into two teams; arrange chairs or standing room as far apart from each other as possible so the opposite team cannot hear; each team elects a recorder to list their ideas.

g. Allow about fifteen minutes for each team to complete their lists and then re-convene.

h. Position teams in chairs, or standing in two lines, facing each other, Team A and Team B.

i. Teams take turns reading statements to each other and responding.
Each "turn" involves these actions:
- The first person from Team A reads the first statement on their list.
- The first person on Team B replies with a rebuttal or positive statement.
- Then the first person from Team B reads the first statement on their list.
- The first person on Team A replies with a rebuttal or positive statement.

  Example

  (Statement) "You should only wear the very latest style jeans".

  (Rebuttal) "It's more important to wear jeans that compliment you and your budget".
- The lists are passed along, e.g. the second persons on Teams A and B read their statements to each other and reply, etc. until twelve statements on each list are addressed.

IV. Enrichment Activities

a. Provide pencils, markers, sports and fashion magazines, scissors, glue and chart paper.

b. Teens make a group poster showing unrealistic expectations.

c. Teens take turns adding, crossing out or altering the photos to make the models more representative of real people.

d. Ask teens what they can do if they want healthier bodies.

Examples
- Determine their body build and set realistic goals.
- Focus on healthy foods and daily exercise involving activities they enjoy.
- Consult a school nurse or medical professional if necessary.

MENTAL DIVERSITY 3

*I am an invisible man. I am a man of substance, of flesh and bone,
fiber and liquids — and I might even be said to possess a mind.
I am invisible, understand, simply because people refuse to see me.*
~ Ralph Ellison

Let's

U	N	-	S	T	I	G	M	A	-	T	I	Z	E

Emotional Issues

Volunteers #1 wait outside the room. Volunteers #2 and people in the room follow the instructions below.

EXPERIMENT #1

Volunteer #1 walks in and the group looks at the person, the group members whisper to each other and they all snicker.

Volunteer #2 asks Volunteer #1 *What did you think when you walked in?*

EXPERIMENT #2

Volunteer #1 walks in and the group yells *Speech! Speech!*
Volunteer #2 asks Volunteer #1 to make a five minute speech. (The volunteer is not expected to speak).
Volunteer #2 asks Volunteer #1 *How did you feel when you walked in and were asked to make a speech?*

EXPERIMENT #3

Volunteer #1 walks in and volunteer #2 says, Y*ou won a big prize.*
Seconds later Volunteer #2 says, *Oh, and I forgot to tell you, you failed a class.*
Volunteer #2 asks Volunteer #1 *How did you feel when I told you that you won a prize? And then how did you feel a few seconds later when I told you that you failed a class?*

Discussion:

1. Were volunteer #1's thoughts and feelings based on real or imaginary situations?
2. Share the story of a time you thought people were against you.
3. Share the story of a time you felt fearful.
4. Share the story of a time you felt happy one minute and sad soon afterward.

Most people have the above experiences some of the time. People with emotional issues may have one or more of these experiences most of the time, and with even more intensity.

5. Are teens with emotional issues and without emotional issues more alike or different? Explain.
6. Why do you think most teens with emotional issues suffer in silence?
7. What would make teens who have emotional issues more willing to share their thoughts and feelings?

Let's UN-STIGMA-TIZE Emotional Issues

FOR THE FACILITATOR

I. Purpose

To understand the commonality of human emotions and diminish the stigma of mental illness.

II. General Comments

For the sake of sensitivity to participants who may have a mental illness, we are using the term "emotional issues." It is the facilitator's choice as to which term to use. Teens fear being perceived as different; the label of mental illness prevents teens from seeking help which can lead to falling grades, failure to reach their maximum potential, substance abuse, self-harm, possible violence, etc. Parents/caregivers who deny or minimize problems, or who do not recognize or understand mental illness, may not want to access treatment or may not know how.

III. Possible Activities

a. Write *Experiment* on the board and recruit three volunteers who are willing to experience some feelings to wait outside the room. These are volunteers #1.

b. Distribute the *Let's Un-stigma-tize Emotional Issues* handout to the remaining teens.

c. Recruit volunteers #2 for each experiment and ask them to follow the instructions. Possible thoughts and feelings experienced by the volunteers are normal emotions but exacerbated by people who have a mental illness (emotional issues).

- Experiment #1 – normal thought – belief that peers are laughing at and talking about the volunteer.
  (emotional issue – prolonged paranoia).
- Experiment #2 – normal emotion – stage fright.
  (emotional issue – prolonged anxiety or fear).
- Experiment #3 – normal emotions – happy then sad.
  (emotional issue – prolonged mood swings).

d. Volunteers take their seats; distribute copies of the handout to volunteers #1.

e. Discussion responses may be written first and then shared or simply discussed aloud.

Possibilities

1. Thoughts and feelings were based on imaginary situations but the intensity was the same as if based on reality; this is often true in psychiatric disorders.
2. 3. 4. Individualized responses.
5. More alike. Explain: Teens with psychiatric disorders experience many of the same thoughts and emotions as teens without disorders but in greater intensity and frequency.
6. They fear peers will distance themselves from them.
7. Teens would seek help if they believed peers, teachers, parents, society would help rather than label or judge them.

IV. Enrichment Activities

a. A delicate but necessary issue - discuss that psychiatric disorders often appear in adolescence, an age when peer approval matters most; a social climate of acceptance can mean the difference between life and death.

b. Ask teens to brainstorm steps a teen with emotional issues might take; a volunteer lists their ideas.

Possibilities

- Share their thoughts and feelings with a trusted adult.
- Consult their physician.
- Possibly take medication if prescribed; know its purpose, side effects and other info.
- Become involved with individual, group and/or family therapy.
- Learn new ways to think and cope.

c. Ask teens what steps they can take to support a friend with emotional issues (listen, show empathy, assure the person you will remain their friend, encourage them to seek help; immediately tell a trusted adult or call 911 or your local emergency services if a peer talks about harming self or others).

My Wellness Scripts

A script is a real or imagined piece of text telling what to say or do in a specific situation. Families, friends, teammates and other cultures have spoken or unspoken rules.

The culture that influences me most is ______________________________

Write your culture's scripts on the illustration below:

Now, write your thoughts about the healthiest way to handle the situations:

My Wellness Scripts

Expressing feelings: ______________________________

Family issues: ______________________________

Social image: ______________________________

Seeking help: ______________________________

Anything else? ______________________________

My Wellness Scripts

FOR THE FACILITATOR

I. Purpose

To understand cultural influences in emotional expression, family issues, social image and seeking help.

II. General Comments

Teens who recognize cultural barriers to mental health are better able to help themselves and others.

III. Possible Activities

a. Encourage teens to think about the many cultures to which they belong (family, peer group, etc.).
b. Ask teens to share their most dominant culture's unwritten rules about showing or holding back feelings.
c. Distribute the *My Wellness Scripts* handout and read aloud the explanations at the top.
d. Explain that scripts are neither right nor wrong and that they vary from culture to culture.
e. Explain that all members of culture may not interpret scripts the same way or comply explicitly.
f. Allow time for completion of the handout.
g. Encourage teens to share their responses.
h. Point out similarities and differences among teens' dominant cultures and scripts.
i. Concepts to discuss:
   - Expressing Feelings – culture suggests the level of holding back or sharing; some cultures see honest expression as healthy, others believe suppression shows self-control.
   - Family Issues – culture suggests whether family secrets are kept at all costs or revealed to save a member's mental health; some cultures expect obedience to family over personal fulfillment (arranged marriages, career directives, etc.).
   - Social Image –some cultures suggest that saving face for the individual and/or family is the highest priority; to admit a problem would bring shame; some see emotional issues as character flaws.
   - Seeking Help – culture suggests whether seeking help signifies strength or weakness; some expect extended family or religious leaders to counsel; some see professionals as outsiders or intruders.

j. Discuss imitation – teens may demonstrate negative or positive thinking based on role models; reactions to emotions are learned (e.g. drink to de-stress or see problems as growth opportunities).
k. Discuss physical complaints – some cultures subconsciously promote transferring emotional pain into headaches, stomach aches or other ailments because these are seen as more socially acceptable.
l. Discuss medication – some cultures expect family support, relaxation, spirituality, nutrition or home remedies to alleviate symptoms; others may expect a medication miracle.
m. Possible responses to *My Wellness Scripts*:
   - Expressing Feelings – share them safely and choose the best possible person, time and place.
   - Family Issues – consider well-intended family advice but explore all options.
   - Social Image – to admit a problem is the first step toward a solution.
   - Seeking Help – select the best sources from among family, friends, clergy and professionals.
   - Anything Else? – responses will vary.

IV. Enrichment Activities

a. Ask teens to share times they received conflicting scripts from different cultures and how they decided which directive to follow.
b. Encourage a discussion about an ethnic match between counselor, teen and family/caregiver; professionals who speak the language and understand the values are better able to help.
c. Encourage a discussion of socio-economic barriers to mental health care – inability to afford treatment, lack of insurance, living in a rural area, caregivers too busy to find resources. Teens need to ask facilitators for assistance in finding local low-cost assistance.

MENTAL ILLNESS MALWARE

Game Show Host Instructions

Read the opening remarks and then pose one question at a time to contestants.
Encourage peers to assist or to add ideas.
After they have responded to a question you may share the parenthesized possibility.

Game Show Host's Opening Remarks

- **Malicious software (malware) is hostile and contaminates computers.**
- **Myths about mental illness and addiction damage people.**
- **When it is your turn I will read a myth and you will refute it with a truthful statement.**
- **You may ask peers for help.**

1. **Mental illness affects only certain types of people.**
   (It occurs in young and old, male and female, rich and poor, regardless of race or ethnicity).
2. **Most people with mental illness are dangerous to society.**
   (Most are not dangerous to others; they are more likely to harm themselves or be harmed).
3. **People with mental illness need to live in hospitals.**
   (With therapy, medication, respect, and equal opportunity they can function well in the community).
4. **Mental illness is caused by poor parenting/care giving.**
   (Chemical imbalances in the brain, heredity and life experiences like trauma often contribute to it).
5. **Teens with mental illness usually get help.**
   (They often do not ask for help because they fear embarrassment or bullying and because of the stigma of mental illness).
6. **People with mental illness can't function well at work.**
   (They are talented and intelligent but often cannot get a job because of the stigma of mental illness.)
7. **People with mental illness don't have successful romantic relationships.**
   (They love and can have families.)
8. **Most medicines for mental illness make people like zombies.**
   (The right meds improve abilities).
9. **Teens can't do anything to help a peer who has mental illness.**
   (They can be a caring friend, encourage the peer to ask for help, respect the person, learn the facts, educate others, and not define the person by the diagnosis).
10. **People can just snap out of it if they try.**
    (They may need meds, therapy, family counseling and support groups).
11. **People who talk about dying by suicide don't really do it.**
    (Many people talk about it, before they actually do it. They may subconsciously be asking for help.)
12. **Addiction is a moral weakness.**
    (It is an illness involving brain chemicals, susceptibility to the substance, culture, etc.)
13. **Addiction is always genetic.**
    (Family history is sometimes involved, but other factors like environment and emotions play a role; addiction can be overcome with treatment).
14. **Alcohol is not as dangerous as drugs.**
    (Alcohol is very dangerous to health and causes deadly accidents).
15. **Addiction is due to weak will-power.**
    (Addiction is a disease; medications, support groups and therapy can help reduce cravings).
16. **Addicts and alcoholics are low class.**
    (People from all financial, ethnic, racial groups and social groups have addictions).

MENTAL ILLNESS MALWARE

FOR THE FACILITATOR

I. Purpose

To refute myths about mental illness and addiction that lead to discrimination.

II. General Comments

Knowledge empowers teens to ask for help if needed and to support peers who have emotional issues.

III. Possible Activities

a. Write *Virus* on the board and ask teens its meaning regarding health and computers (infects people with sickness or interferes with computer operation).
b. Explain that teens will play a non-competitive game about malware. (malicious software)
c. Ask a volunteer to play Game Show Host; give host the *Mental Illness Malware* handout.
d. Review the instructions in the box with the host then direct host to read aloud the Opening Remarks.
e. One by one the host reads a myth and a volunteer contestant refutes it with a truthful statement.
f. The host encourages as many responses as possible before reading the parenthesized possibility.
g. After the game, encourage teens to share other myths or uncertainties they have about mental illness and addiction and to solicit feedback from peers.
h. If unanswered questions arise, provide suggestions and/or refer teens to trusted resources (National Institutes of Health, etc.).

IV. Enrichment Activities

a. Write *Anti-malware* on the board and ask what it does (detects and eradicates unwanted input).
b. Ask teens how they can be human *anti-mental malware* advocates.
   Possibilities
   - Research causes and treatments of mental illness and addiction.
   - Ask parents/caregivers about family history to discourage secrets about these conditions.
   - Conduct an internet search about famous people who experienced emotional or addiction issues.
   - Encourage people with problems to seek professional help.
   - Create inspirational cards to send to a local adolescent or children's psychiatric unit.
   - Research ways to support organizations like NAMI – The National Alliance on Mental Illness.
   - Check out the Strength Of Us website developed by NAMI to empower young adults.
   - Recognize that teens with and without emotional or addictive illnesses are more alike than different.
   - Realize that most people experience strong emotions or excesses in some area (too much technology etc.); people with diagnoses have similar but exaggerated experiences.
c. Ask teens about the most dangerous myth: *people who talk about killing themselves don't.*
   - Explain that most people who commit suicide have shared their thoughts.
   - Ask teens what they would do if a peer revealed thoughts about harming self or others.
   - Elicit that to tell a trusted adult is to save a life; do not be sworn to secrecy.
d. Write the following quotation on the board:

   I am an invisible man.
   I am a man of substance, of flesh and bone, fiber and liquids –
   and I might even be said to possess a mind.
   I am invisible, understand, simply because people refuse to see me. ~ Ralph Ellison

e. Ask teens why they think people refused to see the character (the novelist wrote his feelings as an African American but any culture or individual may feel invisible).
f. Encourage a discussion of ways teens with emotional or learning difficulties are often ignored and ways to acknowledge them (include in conversations and activities, ask their opinions, etc.).

Recognize Your Own Waterloo

In an 1815 battle, Napoleon Bonaparte was defeated outside the Belgian town of Waterloo. Today, the word *waterloo* refers to anything that is difficult to master.

Please answer the following test questions. The use of technology is prohibited.

Translate the following into English:

Wie fühlt es werden Unausgeglichenheit um zu verstehen?

____

Solve this simple math word problem:

Что такое один плюс один?

Answer = ______________________________

1. How did you feel when you tried to answer the questions?

____

____

2. How would you feel if everyone else knew the answers and you didn't?

____

____

3. How would you feel if people laughed because you had trouble with the questions?

____

____

4. What would you hope peers would do in this situation?

____

____

5. Describe a time when you were insensitive to someone's difficulty.

____

____

6. What will you do in the future around people who learn differently than you learn?

____

____

Recognize Your Own Waterloo

FOR THE FACILITATOR

I. Purpose

To experience cognitive difficulty and develop empathy for people with similar challenges.

II. General Comments

Teens consider that feelings and needs are similar despite differences in abilities and that people with limits in one area may be skilled in other areas.

III. Possible Activities

a. Write on the board the following subjects: *Quantum Physics* and *Thermodynamics.*
b. Tell teens they will be tested on one of the subjects.
c. Ask teens to vote for the test topic they prefer.
d. Ask teens how they feel about the upcoming test (concerned, anxious, fearful of failure, etc.).
e. Encourage teens to identify subjects they learn easily and those with which they have difficulty Elicit that different people have different abilities (musical, artistic, linguistic, mathematical, etc.).
f. Explain that teens will take a test but it is not about Quantum Physics or Thermodynamics.
g. Ask a volunteer to read the top two sentences aloud from the *Recognize Your Own Waterloo* handout.
h. Distribute the *Recognize Your Own Waterloo* handouts to the group.
i. Teens are not allowed to use technology to translate.
j. Allow time for completion.
k. Teens are not expected to know the translation from German to English *(How does it feel to be unable to understand?)* and the answer to the Russian math question *(What is one plus one?).*
l. If some teens do know the translations encourage peers to applaud their abilities.
m. Encourage teens to share their responses to the questions under the test in the box on the handouts.

   Possibilities

   1. frustrated
   2. embarrassed, inferior
   3. hurt
   4. help me learn, understand my difficulty
   5. teens may share times they excluded or snickered at a person with fewer skills
   6. help them, understand their struggles

n. Encourage a discussion about people with limitations in one area having talents in another (Walt Disney was slow in school and became a famous movie producer and cartoonist and Alonzo Clemons had a brain injury but started sculpting animals during his childhood).
o. Ask for a show of hands of people who have a *waterloo.* (Explain that everyone has strengths and limitations, no one knows everything.)

IV. Enrichment Activities

a. Ask teens to brainstorm their top three wishes; a volunteer lists them on the board.
b. Ask teens what they think would be the top three wishes of teens with learning difficulties or related challenges (they would be very similar to the typical teens' wants and needs).
c. Encourage discussion and debate about whether teens with special learning needs are better served in regular classrooms, in special classes or in regular classrooms part of the time and in resource classrooms for extra assistance part of the time.
d. Ask about the benefits of the regular classroom for teens with challenges (they are in the least restrictive environment, ideally will find social acceptance and academic growth).
e. Encourage teens to identify ways students who do not face learning difficulties benefit from classes with peers who have varying abilities (frequent, meaningful and positive interactions between people with differences result in changed attitudes; new friendships are likely).

SOCIAL DIVERSITY 4

Who sees all beings in his own Self, and his Self in all beings, loses fear.

~ THE ISHA UPANISHAD

Stories of Hate and Hope

Nazi Annihilation

Hated by Nazis, hidden in the Secret Annex, a Jewish teen in 1940's Europe poured out her fears, hopes and dreams in her diary. *"When I write, I can shake off all my cares."* ... *"It's a wonder I haven't abandoned all my ideals, they seem so absurd and impractical. Yet I cling to them because I still believe, in spite of everything, that people are truly good at heart."* ... *"I hear the approaching thunder that, one day, will destroy us too. I feel the suffering of millions. And yet, when I look up at the sky, I somehow feel that everything will change for the better, that this cruelty too shall end, that peace and tranquility will return once more."*

Just when she thought she and her family would be freed, they were captured and sent to a death camp. Only her dad survived and he made sure *The Diary of a Young Girl* was published.

She wrote, *"I don't want to have lived in vain."* She did not.

Rwandan Revenge

His Tutsi mother was murdered; his Hutu father died trying to protect her. His parents' ethnic groups were at war. Each side of the family saw him as the enemy. Teens like him, of mixed ethnicity, felt out of place and often emphasized one side of their ethnicity while minimizing or hiding the other.

Another sixteen year old who lost his parents in the 1990s Rwanda genocide said *"We can't forget what happened but we are looking forward. My motivation is not having doubt that I will realize my dreams. I want to be someone who is very strong and I want to be somebody... maybe a great singer."*

Commonalities

What was similar about the three teens' circumstances?

____

____

What traits did they have in common?

____

____

Your Story

Write or orally tell a modern day story about you, someone you know, or a fictitious teen.

Describe the environment of bigotry.

Share the character's feelings.

Quote the character's spoken words that suggest hope amidst hate.

Stories of Hate and Hope

FOR THE FACILITATOR

I. Purpose

To identify with victims of genocide and their families; to realize that many of today's teens face deadly dangers emotionally and possibly physically; to develop empathy for targets of discrimination.

II. General Comments

Storytelling impacts the speaker and listener as words and gestures stir up imagination and emotions.

III. Possible Activities

Oral Storytelling Option (recommended)

a. Before session photocopy two *Stories of Hate and Hope* handouts and recruit two storytellers.
b. Allow the storytellers time to pre-read and familiarize themselves with the narratives.
c. When session starts ask for examples of fairy tales, urban legends, myths (accept any responses).
d. Ask teens to define a biography (an account of someone's life) and autobiography (account of one's own life).
e. Explain that teens will hear two stories and will then tell fictional or true stories.
f. Emphasize that listening is vital to create mental images of the people and scenes described.
g. One storyteller reads the Anne Frank story; the other volunteer reads the Rwandan boys' stories aloud.
h. The second volunteer then asks the two *Commonalities* questions and elicits responses.
   Possibilities
   Question #1. They were victims of prejudice in life and death crises.
   Question #2. They had hope and positive plans for their lives.
i. Copy the instructions from the *Your Story* box onto the board.
j. Ask teens to brainstorm examples of bigotry that are not connected with wars.
   Possibilities
   - Bullying
   - Excluding people because of looks, gender, sexual orientation, disability, race, religion, etc.
k. Discuss that both in Europe and Rwanda genocide occurred (attempted killing of all the people from a national, ethnic or religious group).
l. Ask if *killing* always relates only to bodies (no because one can be *killed* or harmed emotionally).
m. Encourage teens to write outlines and quoted statements on paper and to prepare to tell their stories.
n. Encourage teens to share their stories aloud and receive audience feedback.

Written Option

a. Distribute the *Stories of Hate and Hope* handout to all teens; volunteers read aloud.
b. Teens answer the questions aloud.
c. Allow time to compose written stories.
d. Teens read their stories aloud and receive peer feedback.

IV. Enrichment Activities

a. Point out that ancient civilizations also told stories with songs, drawings on cave walls and/or through rock art.
b. Encourage teens to individually illustrate their stories on large paper.
c. Encourage small groups of teens to make murals depicting the hate and hope theme on large sticky chart paper posted on walls.
d. Ask teens to share the stories told by parents/caregivers, grandparents, etc. about their families, race, ethnicity, etc. If they don't have any stories, encourage them to ask.

The Haves vs. the Have Nots

By ____ *team.*

What It's Like to "Have Not"

The Haves vs. the Have Nots

FOR THE FACILITATOR

I. Purpose

To examine the concept of *the haves vs. the have nots* regarding material resources.

II. General Comments

Teens will consider the fallacy of judging people based on socioeconomic status.

III. Possible Activities

a. Before group, gather supplies into three piles:
A pencil; a pencil plus one bright colored marker; a pencil plus a handful of colored markers.
b. When session begins, divide the group into three teams; teammates sit near each other.
c. Explain that each team will make a poster and may use only the supplies provided; no borrowing.
d. Give one team a pencil, another team a pencil and one bright colored marker, another team a pencil and a handful of colored markers.
e. Give each team one copy of *The Haves vs The Have Nots* handout or the poster paper if available.
f. Direct teams to interpret for themselves and depict what it's like to *have not.*
g. Allow time for poster completion.
h. Ask teens to return to their seats and to respond to the following questions.
Possible responses are in parentheses.
   1. What did you notice about the supplies given to each team? (They were different).
   2. How did you feel if your team had more or fewer materials? (Lucky or at a disadvantage).
   3. Regarding supplies received, what did each team need to do to make the best possible poster? (The best they could with what they had).
   4. What would you think if the team with the pencil and all the markers won a prize? (Unfair).
   5. What would have made it a fair contest? (Everyone sharing the same materials).
   6. In addition to supplies, what did it take to make a poster? (Ideas, working together, creativity).
   7. Does the number of markers or crayons always determine which poster is best? (No, there could be a great poster done in pencil or a poorly drawn multicolored picture).
   8. Encourage teens to share their posters and receive peer feedback.

i. Encourage a discussion about the plight of homeless families (living in a car or shelter, etc.).
j. Promote a discussion about teens who run away (living on the streets, obtaining money for food, etc.).
k. Ask teens to identify what else is lost when people face poverty (insincere friends, pride, etc.).
l. Direct teens to brainstorm priceless traits that do not depend on wealth (intelligence, creativity, self-worth, faith, compassion, talent, love, honesty, reliability, determination, etc.).
m. Elicit examples of false status symbols (the newest cell phone, clothing, boots, etc.).

IV. Enrichment Activities

a. Encourage teens to research examples of people from humble beginnings who contributed greatly to society. Teens may give oral presentations to peers about their findings.
b. Dispel stereotypes about homelessness – tell teens about the homeless man who never took a lesson but his music moves listeners to tears as he plays an old piano at a thrift store.
c. Prompt teens to share other examples of negative stereotypes about people in poverty (lazy, etc.).
d. Discuss negative stereotypes about *The Haves* – that all rich people are greedy or arrogant.
e. Point out that many wealthy people start charities, scholarship funds, etc.
f. Ask teens ways they can share what they have with people who are less fortunate (donate goods and services, recycle plastics and/or initiate a bake sale. Give proceeds to a charity, etc.).

Commonalities – Step Forward

If you have been discriminated against for ________ step forward.

If your favorite school subject is ________ step forward.

If your favorite music genre is ________ step forward.

If your favorite sport is ________ step forward.

If you believe in ________ step forward.

If your favorite social networking site is ________ step forward.

If your favorite author is ________ step forward.

If your favorite video game is ________ step forward.

If ________ step forward.

If your parents were born in another country step forward.

If your birth order is ________ step forward.

If your favorite food is ________ step forward.

If your dream job is ________ step forward.

If you are an only child, step forward

If you have a single parent, step forward.

If you are afraid of ________ step forward.

If you want to go to this college ____________ step forward.

If the adults in your life are separated or divorced step forward.

If you really care about ________ step forward.

Commonalities – Step Forward

FOR THE FACILITATOR

I. Purpose

To identify similarities among teens with cultural differences; to foster the habit of considering commonalities.

II. General Comments

Teens play a game where they physically move toward peers who have similar traits and experiences.

III. Possible Activities

a. Before session place chairs in a circle or in two rows facing each other or arrange standing room adequate for one circle or two parallel lines of teens.
b. Copy one of the callout blank shapes onto the board and write *Callout* in the middle.
c. Explain that teens will play a game in which they will be in a circle (or two rows facing each other).
d. Volunteers will call out phrases and fill in the blanks aloud.
e. Peers will step forward if the statement applies.
f. Write this example on the board *If you have brown hair step forward.*
g. Position teens in chairs or rows.
h. Ask about observable differences among group members (gender, hair color, race, clothing, etc.).
i. Distribute the *Commonalities – Step Forward* handout; teens read the phrase starters silently.
j. Teens take turns calling out a phrase starter and filling in the blank aloud.
Ex. If your birth order is the youngest, (or the oldest, or the middle child) step forward.
k. Low risk phrase starters address favorites; others require more revelation.
Ex. If you have been discriminated against because of your race, etc. step forward.
l. There are a few statements with no blanks to fill in, e.g. *If you are spiritual step forward.*
m. One phrase starter is totally open to teens' interpretations (*If ________*).
n. Teens may use any of the phrase starters more than once (with different *fill in the blank* responses).
o. If a *fill in the blank* statement applies, peers step forward to the center of the circle or toward the opposite row.
p. Encourage teens to notice peers who stepped forward.
q. After each turn, all step back into their original positions.
r. Volunteers continue calling out phrase starters, filling in blanks; peers step forward then back, etc.
s. After the game, ask the following questions; possible responses to elicit are parenthesized
- Ask teens to explain how they were or were not surprised at similarities among group members.
- In what areas were there the most similarities?
- Ask teens to brainstorm other traits they may have in common (enthusiasm, empathy, goals, etc.).
- Ask what message the game conveyed (if we search, we find similarities despite differences).

IV. Enrichment Activities

a. Encourage a discussion about people with differences becoming friends and ask for examples from teens' lives that suggest that opposites attract.
b. Ask teens who took the risk of filling in the blanks how they felt when few or no peers stepped forward (possibly disappointed, possibly okay with being unique).
c. Ask teens who took the risk of filling in the blanks how they felt when several peers stepped forward (felt good to have someone with whom to discuss like experiences).
d. Elicit the basic needs experienced by almost everyone (safety, love and belonging, esteem, reaching one's maximum potential, etc.).

Debunk Gender Stereotypes

1. Dependent	2. Decisive	3. Lenient	4. Unemotional	5. Emotional
6. Independent	7. Rational	8. Authoritative	9. Adventurous	10. Tearful
11. Tough	12. Sensitive	13. Compassionate	14. Sympathetic	15. Strict
16. Strong-willed	17. Gentle	18. Powerful	19. Sentimental	20. Forceful
21. Vulnerable	22. Dominant	23. Submissive	24. Supportive	25. Nurturing

Debunk Gender Stereotypes

FOR THE FACILITATOR

I. Purpose

To debunk gender stereotypes by assigning traditionally male or female attributes to the opposite sex.

II. General Comments

In our world many stereotypes exist. We have come a long way in recognizing them, however some people still adhere to false or unfair beliefs about others. Teens will dispute, influence and change the old notions about traits and occupations and will consider how toys and video games have promoted gender generalizations.

III. Possible Activities

a. Before session, cut the *Debunk Gender Stereotypes* handout on the broken lines; stack cutouts face down. Option: Provide a poster with a male photo, a poster with a female photo and scotch tape.

b. Ask for a volunteer to make up a sentence where a traditional masculine male wears pink.
Ex. The handsome quarterback's pink shirt showed his abs.

c. Explain that teens will pick up cutouts and state the word's association with males or females. If posters are used (III.a.) teens tape the cutouts on the poster they believe the word describes.

d. Teens will then compose a sentence where the word applies to the opposite sex; peers may help.

e. Teens take turns at the front of the room, writing the cutout words on the board (or taping them on the posters) and stating sentences.

Possibilities	(m) or (f) shows the **stereotyped** gender; italicized sentences exemplify the **opposite**.
Dependent	(f) *The jock was dependent on teammates for help when he broke his leg.*
Decisive	(m) *The female model was decisive when she turned down ads for cigarettes.*
Lenient	(f) *The male teacher was lenient when students forgot their homework.*
Unemotional	(m) *The aunt was unemotional when relatives tried to manipulate her for money.*
Emotional	(f) *An auto body repairman became emotional when he saw his car had hit a deer.*
Independent	(m) *The female student made an independent choice to pursue a career in math.*
Rational	(m) *The girlfriend made a rational decision to end the abusive relationship.*
Authoritative	(m) *The female caregiver was authoritative when she set curfews for her teens.*
Adventurous	(m) *The female boxer was adventurous when she took on the former champion.*
Tearful	(f) *The hockey player was tearful when his teammate was badly injured.*
Tough	(m) *The female coach was tough when she disciplined drug-takers.*
Sensitive	(f) *The male construction worker was sensitive to his partner's feelings.*
Compassionate	(f) *The male pitcher was compassionate when asked to represent a charity.*
Sympathetic	(f) *The father was sympathetic when his son lost the choir competition.*
Strict	(m) *The mother was strict about getting the yard work finished.*
Strong-willed	(m) *The female band director was strong-willed when she insisted on extra practice.*
Gentle	(f) *The male soldier fought tough in battle but was gentle toward his dog.*
Powerful	(m) *The female senator was a powerful advocate for human rights.*
Sentimental	(f) *The male professor became sentimental when he read poetry to the class.*
Forceful	(m) *The female teen wrote forceful lyrics to defend victims of bullying.*
Vulnerable	(f) *The male was vulnerable to humiliation when bullies insulted him.*
Dominant	(m) *The female debater was a dominant force on the team.*
Submissive	(f) *The male hiker was submissive to guidelines by his leader.*
Supportive	(f) *The male musician was supportive when he taught teens at no charge.*
Nurturing	(f) *The stay at home male caregiver was nurturing toward his children.*

f. Ask teens to describe how they will portray at least one trait that was stereotypically attributed to the opposite gender.

IV. Enrichment Activities

Follow up with *Gender Stereotypes – Toys and Traditions*, page 65

Gender Stereotypes
Toys and Traditions

In our world, many stereotypes exist.
We have come a long way, however some people still stick to these old, false, unfair ideas.
Brainstorm an item for each category and the message it conveys.

A Traditional Boy Toy	A Traditional Girl Toy	A Male Stereotype in Video Games	A Female Stereotype in Video Games	A Traditional Male Occupation	A Traditional Female Occupation
The Message	**The Message**	**The Message**	**The Message**	**The Message**	**The Message**

Imagine how you can …

Dispute one old idea.

____

____

____

____

Change or influence one of the stereotypes.

____

____

____

____

Gender Stereotypes – Toys and Traditions

FOR THE FACILITATOR

I. Purpose

To highlight messages promoted by toys, video games and traditional occupational expectations.

II. General Comments

Teens are encouraged to refute stereotypical ideas and initiate change.

III. Possible Activities

a. Distribute the *Toys and Traditions* handout, page 65.

Team Option (recommended)

Divide teens into six teams and assign one of the categories to each; teammates sit together.

Each team elects a writer to list all of their ideas on the handout.

Allow time for completion.

The group re-convenes and the writers present their teams' lists to peers.

Individual Option

Teens complete the handout independently then share their ideas.

Possibilities

Traditional Boy Toys	Traditional Girl Toys	Male Stereotypes in Video Games	Female Stereotypes in Video Games	Traditional Male Occupations	Traditional Female Occupations
weapons vehicles building sets tools soldiers doctors firemen policemen	toy ovens dishes/cookware cleaning items hair styling sets jewelry making baby dolls mermaids princesses fashion dolls	action figures power figures warriors superheroes	curvy skimpy clothes maybe victims maybe violent	surgeons lawyers mechanics electricians astronauts chemists professors administrators	nurses secretaries teachers payroll clerks social workers caregivers housekeepers
The Message	**The Message**	**The Message**	**The Message**	**The Message**	**The Message**
Men are doers; they build, repair, fight and rescue, etc.	Women cook, clean, care for children and must be beautiful.	Aggression is manly.	Sexuality, victimization and violence are glamorous.	Men are capable and in charge; most are highly skilled.	Women are assistants, nurturers, and less likely to be in charge.

b. Imagine how you can…

- Dispute one old idea (women can be surgeons, males can be nurses, etc.).
- Change or influence one of the stereotypes (tell a younger brother it's ok to play with cooking items; pursue a non-traditional career; contact toy and video game manufacturers about providing more gender-neutral products and advertising).

IV. Enrichment Activities

a. Ask teens to share childhood experiences of being encouraged or discouraged to play with certain toys.

b. Ask teens to share their career goals, particularly if they contradict the stereotyped gender for the job.

c. Encourage a discussion about society's efforts to stop stereotyping (some toy stores are promoting and advertising gender neutral items; movies show more males are becoming stay-at-home caregivers; many television shows are casting females in roles of physicians and attorneys, etc.).

Jump into the Act

THE LUNCH BUNCH

Cast of 4 includes Narrator, Petrina, Peer #1 and Peer #2.

Narrator: *"Petrina looks and dresses differently and is very quiet; she eats alone in the cafeteria."*
Petrina: Sits away from peers and pretends to eat lunch.
Peer #1: *"I think we should ask her to sit with us. She's probably lonely."*
Peer #2: *"Leave her alone, she's weird."*
Narrator: *Who can jump into the act and make a positive difference?"*

THE BADMOUTH BULLIES

Cast of 5 includes Narrator, Victim, Bullies #1 and #2 and Bystander.

Narrator: *"People are making ethnic, racial or sexual orientation slurs."*
Victim: Sits in a slumped position, hands over ears.
Bully #1: *"You no good, typical, disgusting thing!"*
Bully #2: *"Yeah! You no good, typical, disgusting thing!"*
Bystander: Shakes head as if to silently say "No" but puts hand over own mouth.
Narrator: *"Who can jump into the act and make a positive difference?"*

THE PITIFUL PARTY

Cast of 3 includes Narrator, Partygoer #1 and Partygoer #2.

Partygoer #1: *"Look at these cell phone pictures of Brittany. She was drunk at Saturday's party."*
Partygoer #2: *"She was passed out and guys were making out with her."*
Partygoer #1: *"Let's send the pictures to everyone who knows her."*
Narrator: *"Who can jump into the act and make a positive difference?"*

THE UNFRIENDLY FAN

Cast of 3 includes Narrator, Victim of Discrimination and Fan.

Narrator: *"This act involves a member of a minority who wants to go to a game with peers."*
Victim of Discrimination: *"I'd really like to go to the game tonight but I don't have a ride."*
Fan #1: *"Sorry but my friends and I don't have any room in our cars."*
Narrator: *"Who can jump into the act and make a positive difference?"*

THE BLAME GAME

Cast includes Narrator, Player and Different Culture Player.

Narrator: *"This act involves a player being blamed."*
Player: *"You people just don't know how to play this game. You caused us to lose."*
Different Culture Player: *"I feel so guilty."*
Narrator: *"Who can jump into the act and make a positive difference?"*

EMBARRASSED

Cast of 3 includes Narrator, Emily and Questionable Friend.

Emily: *"They're spreading my pictures around. I was half dressed and didn't know what I was doing."*
Questionable Friend: *"You asked for it by getting drunk. Just pretend you don't care and they'll stop."*
Narrator: *"Who can jump into the act and make a positive difference?"*

Jump into the Act

FOR THE FACILITATOR

I. Purpose

To take action to make a positive difference in a bullying, blaming or discrimination situation.

II. General Comments

In this type of theater the viewers become actors, but must play teens (not teachers, parents, etc.).

III. Possible Activities

a. Before session make five photocopies of the *Jump into the Act* handout and cut on the broken lines.

b. Place each *Act* into a stack of scripts.

c. Recruit four actors for *The Lunch Bunch* and distribute their scripts.

d. Allow them to briefly practice in the hall outside the group room.

e. While the cast members practice, read these directions to the audience:

You will see an act; when asked, one or more viewers may enter the scene and intervene as a teen, not an adult, and make a positive difference. Emphasize, *This should be done briefly, with one or two actions or lines of dialogue.* (This prevents the act from becoming too long and complicated).

f. The *Lunch Bunch* performs and audience intervenes.

Ex: An audience member enters the act saying *Let's include her* or sits near Petrina and converses.

g. After the act, audience claps and the cast stays at the front of the room for questions and answers.

h. Ask each actor how it felt to play the role.

i. Ask the audience about other ways the act could have played out.

j. Each of the remaining acts proceeds similarly (a different cast receive scripts, practice and perform; audience intervenes; lastly, ask the same questions of the actors and audience).

k. After all the acts have been performed encourage a discussion.

Ideas to Elicit

- In real life one can intervene to be an ally and to stop discrimination, etc.
- Report the spread of unkind texts, embarrassing photos and discrimination to a counselor, parent, or trusted adult (anonymously if necessary); to stand by silently suggests complicity.
- Persons who listen to gossip, look at compromising photos, repeat or forward damaging content are as responsible for perpetuating pain as the instigator.
- To ignore sexting does not make it go away.
- Sexting is illegal in many circumstances.
- Bullies and excluders seek popularity and power through hurting people.
- True friendships are based on loyalty and mutual respect.
- To accept and include people saves lives and makes life worth living.

IV. Enrichment Activities

a. Encourage teens to write brief screenplays and perform for the group or a school-wide audience.

- Suggest that peers bring props.
- Ask artists to design simple sets or scenery and posters.
- Request that writers develop advertising flyers and printed programs.
- Teens may compose questions to ask actors and the audience after each act.
- Encourage a discussion about ways victims can become survivors and empower themselves.

b. Encourage a discussion about ways potential victims can empower themselves (do not re-read mean messages but save as evidence for legal charges; find people with similar interests and values; join a club or team with like-minded peers; obtain help for stress management, assertiveness and self-esteem; do not take others' cruelty personally – recognize that bullies have severe problems, etc.) .

Sexual Orientation

Sexual orientation refers to genetic and gender-associated behaviors as well as to a lasting pattern of emotional, romantic and/or sexual attraction to males, females or both. Some people exclude, bully or dislike people based on sexual orientation.

1. Why might people keep their sexual orientation a secret?

2. What would allow people to state their sexual orientation openly?

3. How would you feel if you were discriminated against because of your sexual orientation?

4. If same sex romance is not for you, how can you accept others' rights to these relationships?

5. Sexual orientation is only one part of personhood.
   In what ways do you think teens with different sexual orientations are similar?

6. Circle and share your interpretation of one bumper sticker below:
   a. *Straight but not narrow.*
   b. *Live and let live.*
   c. *Be careful who you hate. It could be someone you love.*
   d. *Hate free zone.*
   e. *Love is louder.*

7. Create your own bumper sticker promoting tolerance for different sexual orientations.

Sexual Orientation

FOR THE FACILITATOR

I. Purpose

To encourage acceptance of diverse sexual orientations.

II. General Comments

Sexual orientation is one of the reasons teens exclude and bully. Teens are encouraged to acknowledge people's rights to relationships with the same, opposite or both sexes. The goal is not to promote sexual activity or any specific agenda but to reduce prejudice and discrimination toward people with beliefs different from their own.

III. Possible Activities

Roving Reporter Format

(recommended only if your population can handle the subject respectfully).

a. Recruit a volunteer roving reporter; provide the *Sexual Orientation* handout to the teen.
b. Ask the group about the duties of a roving reporter (asks controversial questions and expects short comments from various people with varying responses).
c. Explain that the roving reporter will read some information and ask questions.
d. The reporter will go around the room soliciting a few responses to each question.
e. There are no right or wrong responses; only personal opinions are requested.
f. People will raise hands if they want to answer; no one will be asked to share.
g. The roving reporter reads the info in the box at the top of the page, then asks the first question in the box.
h. After a few teens have responded the reporter proceeds through number 5; teens respond.
i. The reporter is thanked and is seated.
j. Distribute the *Sexual Orientation* handout; allow time for completion of numbers 6 and 7.
k. Encourage teens to share their responses.

Individual Format

(suggested if some teens would be uncomfortable with the reporter format).

a. Distribute the *Sexual Orientation* handout; a volunteer reads the info in the top box of the page aloud.
b. Explain there are no right or wrong answers; only personal opinions are requested.
c. Assure participants they may keep their responses private or share them with the group.
d. Allow time for completion; encourage teens to share responses within their comfort zones.

IV. Enrichment Activities

Ask teens to brainstorm related questions for a roving reporter and possible responses.

Examples

a. What is the significance of a same sex crush in early teen years?
(May relate to hormones and experimentation and does not mean the person will continue to have those feelings.)
b. What would help people who are unsure of their sexual orientation?
(Give it time to evolve.)
c. What can one do if one is in fear of parent/caregivers' reactions to their sexual orientation?
(Talk first with a trusted family member or counselor.)
d. What can one do if a person is being bullied or rejected because of sexual orientation?
(Tell a trusted adult, ask for support system resources.)
e. What can one do if depressed or stressed about sexual orientation issues?
Talk with a school counselor, spiritual advisor, physician or other trusted adult.)

The Tip of the Iceberg

Consider the group of people you are most likely to stereotype based on their culture. Culture pertains to similar behavior, values, beliefs and/or characteristics of a particular group of people and may relate to age, body size/image, disability, ethnicity, family, gender, neighborhood, race, religion, sexual orientation, social subculture, spiritual, status or other common bonds.

Identify the group with a code name: ____________________

Start at the bottom layer *My Thoughts* and work upward to *My Actions*.

My negative thoughts and actions — Iceberg A

My positive thoughts and actions — Iceberg B

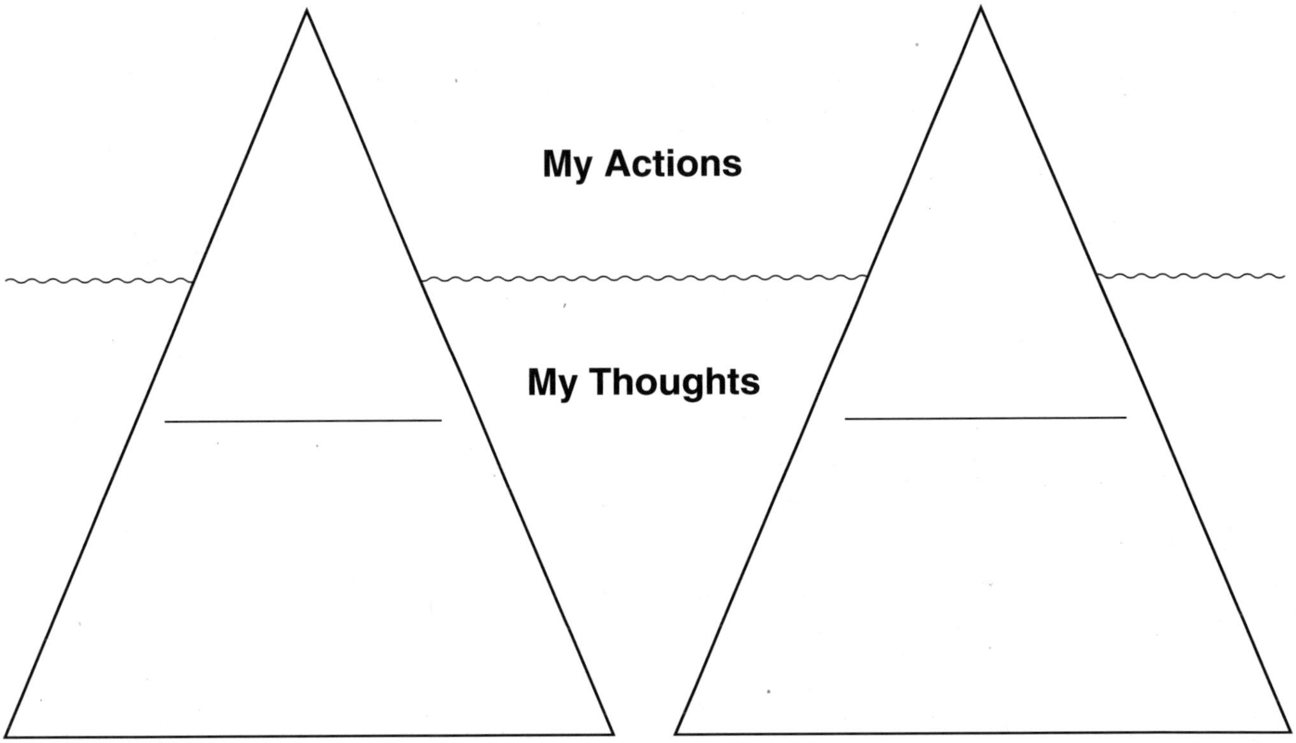

ONLY A SMALL PORTION OF AN ICEBERG IS ABOVE WATER.

Why are actions just the tip of the iceberg? ____

____

Which iceberg is cold-hearted and closed-minded? ________

Which iceberg is warm-hearted and open-minded? ________

Which iceberg would you want to meet if you were a member of the certain culture? ________

Which iceberg do you want to be? ________

How can you *unthaw* Iceberg A? ____

____

____

The Tip of the Iceberg

FOR THE FACILITATOR

I. Purpose

To expose thought patterns that underlie stereotyping, prejudice and discrimination toward different cultures.

II. General Comments

Teens will recognize underlying motivations for positive or negative actions toward a culture.

III. Possible Activities

a. If possible display a few internet photos of icebergs and point out their tips and layers.
b. Ask teens what is meant by the *tip of the iceberg* (the evident part of something largely hidden).
c. Distribute *The Tip of the Iceberg* handout.
d. Ask a volunteer to read the text above the icebergs aloud.
e. Allow time for completion.
f. Note that teens need to conceal identity of the group they are likely to stereotype by using a code name.
g. Encourage teens to share their responses.

Possibilities

Iceberg A	*Iceberg B*
I am part of an in-group; they're outcasts.	I've worked or played with the members.
I see few similarities between my group and theirs.	I find common bonds with almost anyone.
I have little contact with members of this group.	I recognize individual differences in the members.
I think all members of this group are the same.	I believe in fairness.
I believe people's weaknesses keep them down.	I know about environment's impact.
I believe what others tell me about this group.	I form my own opinion about each individual.
I classify people based on their culture.	I'm aware that a person has many components.
I believe people rarely change.	I believe people often change.

1. Actions are the visible tip but they are motivated by underlying thoughts.
2. *Iceberg A*
3. Iceberg B
4. *Iceberg B*
5. Ideally teens will choose *Iceberg B*; if some choose *Iceberg A*, do not engage in a debate.
6. Unthaw *Iceberg A* by thinking *I'll treat people as I want to be treated* (and varied responses).

IV. Enrichment Activities

Ask teens to brainstorm other icebergs' tips and underlying motives.

Examples

- Tip – gossiping – motive: to appear in-the-know and important by spreading stories
- Tip – bullying – motive: to gain power through inflicting pain
- Tip – bragging – motive: to look good by exaggerating accomplishments or possessions
- Tip – racist, sexist, insulting jokes – motive: to appear funny or cool at someone else's expense
- Tip – anger – motives: fear, loss of esteem, loss of control over a situation or abandonment
- Tip – laughing at someone who is different – motive: ignorance (how to treat the person)

Multifaceted Gems

Gems have many facets, geometrically arranged flat surfaces that bring out the stone's brilliance.

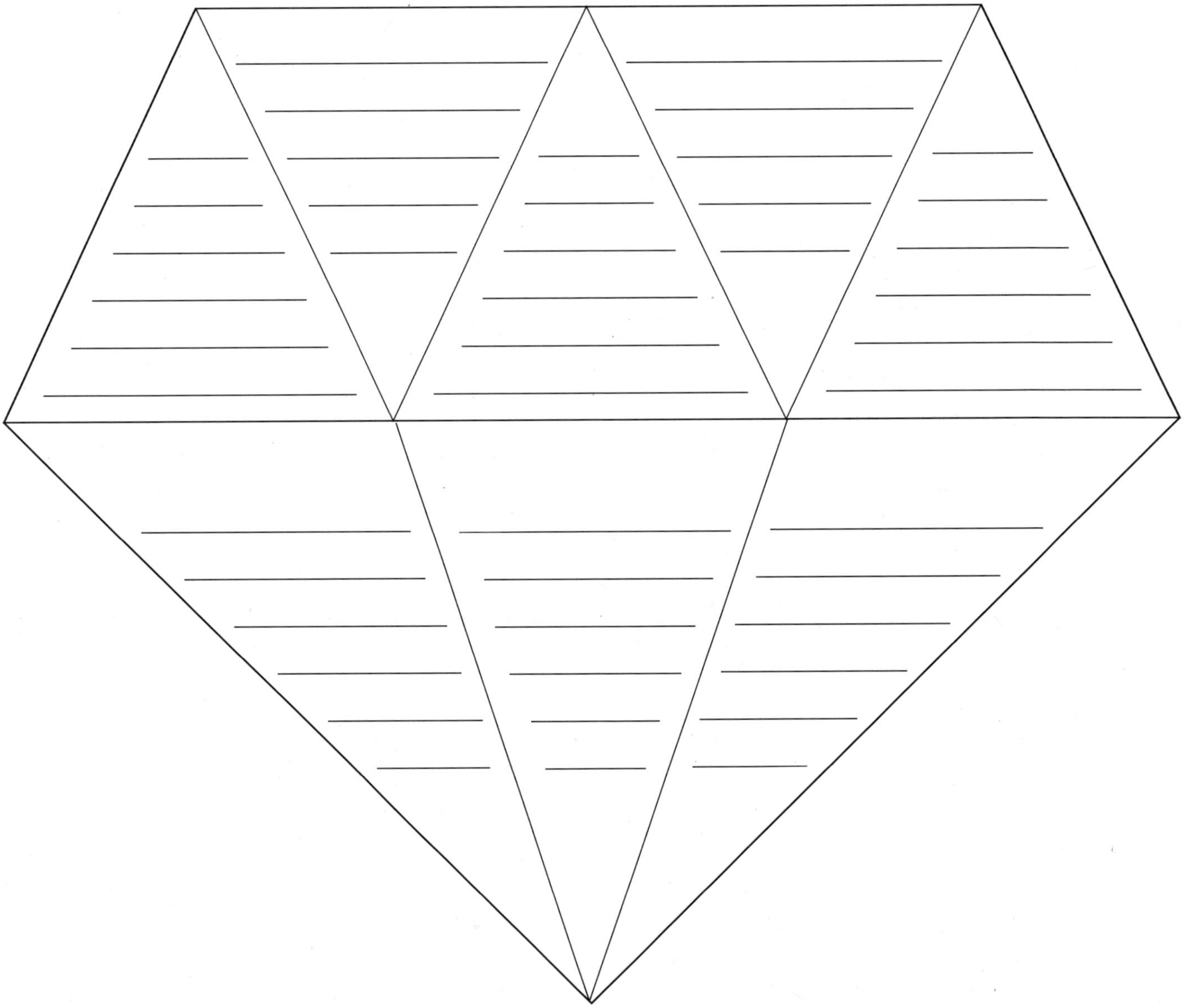

You are a treasure with many positive characteristics!
"Don't ever let anyone dull your sparkle."

Choose eight of your positive characteristics that are most important to you and write one on each facet.

On the back of this page, elaborate about one or more of your facets.

Give yourself a fictitious name. ____

You will choose whether to reveal your true identity in a game that follows.

Multifaceted Gems

FOR THE FACILITATOR

I. Purpose

To view self and others as complex individuals rather than labeling people for one facet, e.g. race.

II. General Comments

Teens describe their own multifaceted identities, then play a guessing game to learn more about peers.

III. Possible Activities

a. Ask teens to show gemstones they may be wearing; alternatively show photos of cut gems.
b. Write *Multifaceted* on the board and ask its meaning (many-sided, complex).
c. Distribute the *Multifaceted Gems* handout and ask volunteers to read the text aloud.
d. Allow time for completion.
e. Facets may include different cultures: similar behavior, talents. values, beliefs and/or characteristics of a particular group of people and may relate to age, body (shape, size, and weight), disability, ethnicity, family, gender, race, religion, sexual orientation, social, spiritual, status or other common bonds.
f. Explain that teens will play a guessing game about identities.
g. Remind teens they used fictitious names and can choose whether to reveal their identities.
h. Allow teens who do not want their handouts read aloud to keep them.
i. Collect and shuffle the papers from teens who volunteer to play.
j. Teens take turns in front of the room picking up a handout and reading the facets and fictitious names aloud.
k. Peers guess the owner's identity.
l. Teens who acknowledge their identities may read aloud their elaborations about one of their traits.

IV. Enrichment Activities

a. Ask teens to identify new information they learned about peers.
b. Point out that gems are covered in dirt during the mining process.
c. Ask teens to brainstorm conditions that conceal people's identities.
   Possibilities
   - Labels
   - Stereotypes
   - Damaging gossip
   - Focusing on one trait to the exclusion of others e.g. a person's nationality
   - Fear of rejection or being judged if one reveals true characteristics
d. Ask teens how learning about people's many facets breaks down barriers.
   Possibilities
   - Similarities may emerge.
   - Unique qualities are appreciated.
   - Empathy may increase as background information is revealed.
e. Encourage teens to brainstorm ways people try to dull their sparkle and how they can be sure not to ever let anyone dull their sparkle.
f. If possible, provide small, shiny, *gemstones,* to participants, to remind them of their brilliance.

Sub-Cultures that Sub-Merge

A subculture is a group of people whose behavior and beliefs are different from the larger culture.

What do you think motivates most people to become involved in subcultures?

____

Some subcultures, like undertows, cause members to sink.

Check boxes next to groups you have joined or are tempted to join:

❑ Bullies
❑ Drinkers
❑ Drug users
❑ Excessive overeaters
❑ Gamblers
❑ Game sites that consume players
❑ Partners in crime
❑ People who sell their bodies
❑ Porno participants
❑ Self-injurers
❑ Sext-ers
❑ Shop 'til you drop spenders
❑ Smokers
❑ Social networks that drag people down
❑ Other ______________________
❑ Other ______________________

Next to each statement below, write the number of the item you are referring to above, and on the line below, substitute a non-judgmental response.

1. It could never happen to me. ___ ______________________________
2. I'd never do that. ___ ______________________________
3. I'm not like them. ___ ______________________________
4. Look at those people. ___ ______________________________
5. They're disgusting. ___ ______________________________
6. Finish this thought on the illustration below. ***I have a heart to help by …***

Sub-Cultures that Sub-Merge

FOR THE FACILITATOR

I. Purpose

To understand what motivates teens to join negative subcultures; to replace criticism with compassion.

II. General Comments

In addition to biological and psychological factors, peers can greatly influence adolescent behavior.

III. Possible Activities

a. Read this scenario to teens:
   As I was ordering my drive-through meal, I overheard a teen telling a co-worker…
   "There's a homeless dumpster diver near the trash bin. He is eating our garbage. I'm afraid of him".
b. Ask teens their impressions about the worker's comments (negative label, unfounded fear).
c. Display a container of water and ask a volunteer to hold a pencil down under water.
d. Ask teens how people can be immersed in something (smothering relationships, addictions, etc.).
e. Encourage a discussion about why teens become involved in subcultures.
   Possibilities
   - A sense of belonging
   - A belief that one will have built-in friends
   - Prestige for being a member
   - Acceptance, especially if previously rejected
f. Distribute the *Sub-Cultures that Sub-Merge* handout and ask a volunteer to read the text in the box.
g. Allow time for completion.
h. Encourage teens to share their responses.
   Possibilities corresponding to the numbers on the handout
   1. "That *could* happen to me or anyone else I know."
   2. "I *don't* know what I might do in difficult circumstances."
   3. "I *am* like others in some ways."
   4. "I need to look within *myself*."
   5. "They may have an addiction, feel desperate, need coping skills, etc."
   6. Teens may *have a heart to help by…*
   - Telling a trusted adult about dangerous behaviors.
   - Asking teachers and counselors to provide education about the check-listed subcultures.
   - Joining groups e.g., S.A.D.D. (Students Against Destructive Decisions).
   - Starting a campus campaign (anti-drug, anti-bullying, pro-safety, pro-healthy lifestyles, etc.).

IV. Enrichment Activities

Ask teens to brainstorm other reasons why some teens turn to crime, addiction, prostitution, etc.
Examples
- Some people are biologically and/or emotionally susceptible to substance abuse.
- Role models who drink, use drugs, steal, etc.
- An environment where it seems as if *everybody does it.*
- Poor self-esteem.
- Neglect or rejection by parents/caregivers or peers.

Superlative Subcultures

A subculture is a group of people whose behavior and beliefs are different from the larger culture.

Subcultures can relate to interests and abilities or to helping people.

1. In the box in front of each item, check groups you have joined.
2. In the box in after each item, check groups you would like to join.
3. Put an asterisk (*) on the end line, regarding club(s) or group(s) you would like to start.

- ❑ Academic quiz bowls, math, science . . . ❑ __
- ❑ Art appreciation and artistic creation . . . ❑ __
- ❑ Band, orchestra, composers, lyricists . . . ❑ __
- ❑ Chorus . . . ❑ __
- ❑ Civil freedoms . . . ❑ __
- ❑ Comedy . . . ❑ __
- ❑ Crafts . . . ❑ __
- ❑ Cultural diversity, foreign language . . . ❑ __
- ❑ Dance . . . ❑ __
- ❑ Debate . . . ❑ __
- ❑ Drama . . . ❑ __
- ❑ Games, chess, cards, etc. . . . ❑ __
- ❑ Gay-Straight Alliance . . . ❑ __
- ❑ Key clubs, service organizations . . . ❑ __
- ❑ Music appreciation . . . ❑ __
- ❑ Photography . . . ❑ __
- ❑ Politics . . . ❑ __
- ❑ Science fiction . . . ❑ __
- ❑ Sports, exercise . . . ❑ __
- ❑ Tutoring . . . ❑ __
- ❑ Writing (other) ____________ . . . ❑ __
  - ❑ Stories . . . ❑ __
  - ❑ Poetry . . . ❑ __
  - ❑ Newspaper articles . . . ❑ __
  - ❑ Magazine copy . . . ❑ __
  - ❑ Yearbook copy . . . ❑ __
- ❑ Other ____________ ❑ __
- ❑ Other ____________ ❑ __
- ❑ Other ____________ ❑ __
- ❑ Other ____________ ❑ __

4. What can you, as a club member, do when a new student arrives or someone seems lonely?

____

5. Circle what you believe are the problems in your school.

Abusive Relationships	Academics
Alcohol	Attitude
Bullying	Cheating
Conflicts	Depression
Discipline	Discrimination
Disrespect	Drugs
Gangs	Weapons
Poverty	Other ____________
Other ____________	Other ____________

6. Plan a Positive Peer Subculture Program to help solve the problem(s).

____

____

____

____

Superlative Subcultures

FOR THE FACILITATOR

I. Purpose

To foster involvement in productive groups and promote positive peer subcultures.

II. General Comments

Superlative subcultures prompt teens to pursue their passions with like-minded peers.

III. Possible Activities

a. Ask teens who belong to clubs at school to raise their hands.
b. Encourage teens to identify organizations outside of school (scouts, youth groups, 4 H, gymnastics).
c. Write *Superlative* on the board and ask its meaning (excellent).
d. Distribute the *Superlative Subcultures* handout.
e. Ask volunteers to write these instructions on the board:
   1. Check groups you have joined in first box of each item.
   2. Check groups you would like to join in the box after each item.
   3. Put an asterisk (*) on the end line regarding club(s) or group(s) you would like to start.
f. Allow time for completion.
g. Encourage teens to share their responses.
   Responses to Numbers 1, 2, 3, and 5 are personalized; Number 4 – club members would invite newcomers or lonely students to join or help them find a club related to their interests. Number 6 is addressed below.

IV. Enrichment Activities

a. Suggest that teens who circled the same problems separate into teams. If they chose more than one problem, suggest they go into the group with the fewest number of people.
b. Teammates plan positive peer subculture programs.
c. Each team elects a recorder to list their ideas.

   Possible program components
   - Develop a Purpose Statement
   - Decide: Who, What, Where, When, Why and How?
   - Ask permission from administration
   - Approach potential advisors
   - Plan advertisements to recruit members
   - Plan activities – meetings, guest speakers, create posters and flyers, make announcements, promote awareness of the problem through media
   - Use social networking to solicit solutions
   - Use research techniques to see what works elsewhere
   - Plan special events
   - Organize fund-raising campaigns
   - Other ______________________________

d. If feasible at your facility, motivate teens to actually start the clubs.

EXCEPTIONS TO ACCEPTANCE 5

This is the unusual thing about non-violence—nobody is defeated, and everybody shares in the victory.

~ Dr. Martin Luther King, Jr.

Violent Characters

Free speech bombards you with various voices.

Free choice allows you to select your mindset.

Media violence can create a culture where hurting people is glamorized and rewarded.

Promote a culture of non-violence by engaging in a panel discussion about characters in movies, media, sports, etc. who get away with violence. Prepare for the discussion by writing notes for yourself.

Identify the real life consequences most aggressors face.

List ways to stick up for oneself without physical or verbal violence.

Changing Song Lyrics

Music can incite violence or promote peace.

You can choose what enters your ears and your head.

You decide what to tune out or turn on.

Promote a culture of non-violence by re-writing a current song's lyrics that promotes violence to an anti aggression theme or compose your own message of harmony.

Media Violence Debate

Which came first?

Do violent games cause aggression?

Or, are violence-prone people more likely to make fantasy a reality?

Promote a culture of non-violence by engaging in a debate.
Two people will flip a coin to decide which side to take.
Each person can prepare by writing notes on this paper.

Person #1 argues that violent video games, movies, songs, etc. do not influence behavior.

Person #2 argues that teens with aggressive tendencies seek out and are more affected by violent content and use media to justify their behavior.

School Crime Watch

Is it helpful or harmful to monitor peers?

Citizen patrols exist in some communities.

To what extent can people police themselves?

Promote a culture of non-violence by engaging in a debate.
Two people will flip a coin to decide which side to take.
Each person can prepare by writing notes on this paper.

Person #1 debates the pros of a School Crime Watch in which students patrol the halls, parking lots and campus, and report suspicious behavior.

Person #2 debates the cons of a School Crime Watch in which students patrol the halls, parking lots and campus, and report suspicious behavior.

Playing with Toy Guns

Cops and robbers.

Aliens, predators and power figures.

War games.

Promote a culture of non-violence by engaging in a debate.
Two people will flip a coin to decide which side to take.
Each person can prepare by writing notes on this paper.

Person #1 debates the pros of children playing with toy guns.

Person #2 debates the cons of children playing with toy guns.

Cool Down the Heat of Anger

Anger is understandable.

Things don't always go our way.

We can't control what others do or say.

Promote a culture of non-violence by decorating a door to depict ways to cool down in the heat of anger. Create your draft on this page and then transfer it to a door that will be noticed by other teens.

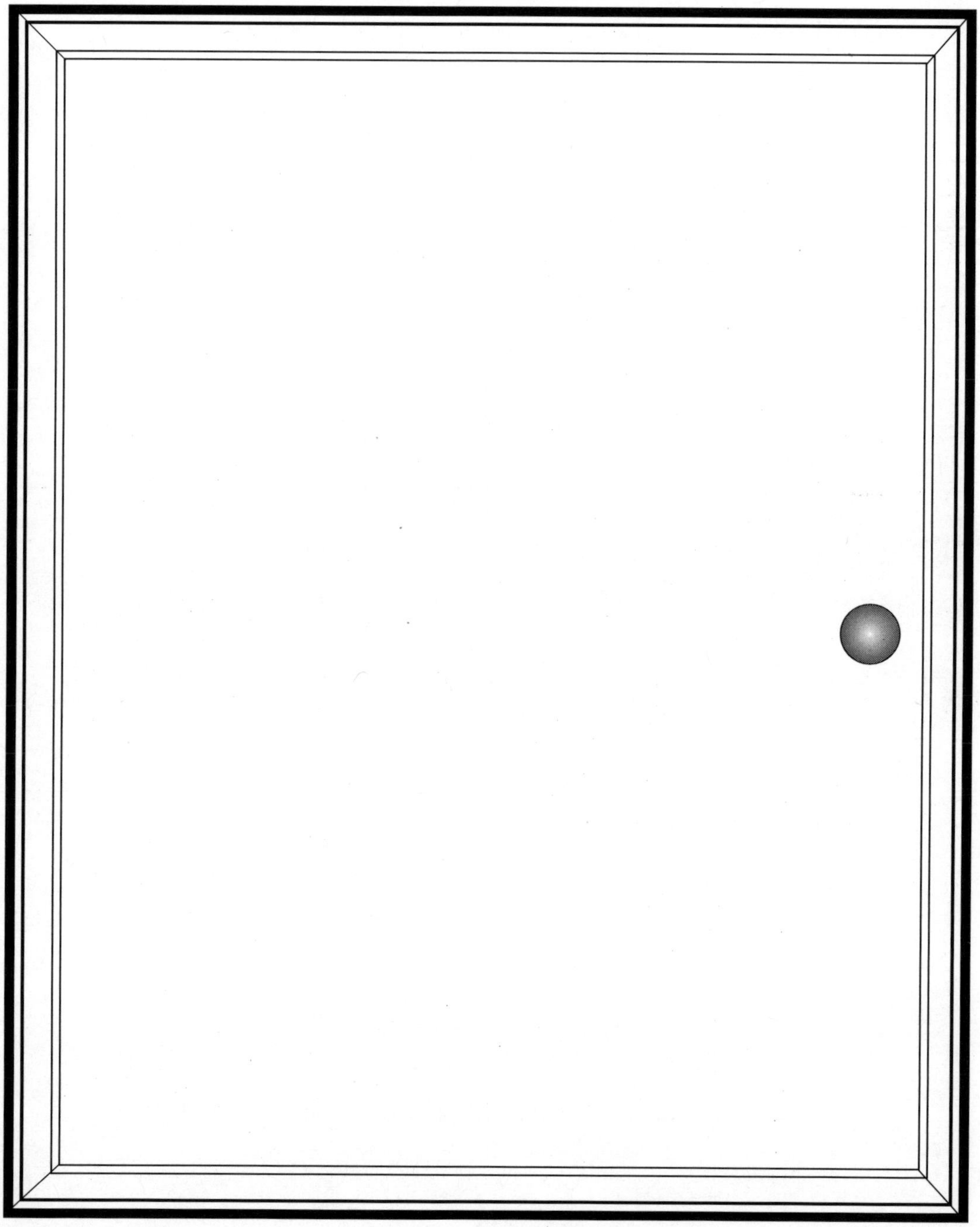

Non-Violence Bumper Stickers

A quick and catchy phrase sticks in the mind.

The message is hard to miss.

Spread the word with your words.

Promote a culture of non-violence by writing several bumper stickers or T-shirt slogans with a message of non-violence in six words or less.
Example: *Stop hate before it's too late*

Peace Poster

"A picture is worth a thousand words."

How about a picture plus words?

How about symbols, cartoons, caricatures, etc.?

Promote a culture of non-violence by drafting a poster promoting peace. Consider enlarging it on poster board and display it in a place where others can see it.

Criticizing Media Violence Poster

Media matters.

Television, radio, newspapers, magazines and the internet inform and influence.

Social networking, photo and video sharing, connect people and ideas.

Promote a culture of non-violence by drafting a poster criticizing media violence. Consider enlarging it on poster board and display it in a place where others can see it.

How Bullying Hurts Me as a Victim

Physical, emotional, verbal, sexual and cyber bullying are ALL an attack!

In what ways can I be beaten down?

What parts of my identity are at risk?

Promote an anti-bullying culture by writing an essay titled *How Bullying Hurts Me* from the point of view of the victim (the person being bullied). Read the essay aloud as a mock video presentation.

How Bullying Hurts Me as a Perpetrator

Physical, emotional, verbal, sexual and cyber bullying are ALL an attack!

Popular culture idealizes power. Violence may be portrayed as strength.

What do I show about me when I lash out?

Promote an anti-bullying culture by writing an essay titled *How Bullying Hurts Me* from the point of view of the perpetrator (the person who bullies). Read the essay aloud as a mock video presentation.

Prevent School Violence

Physical, emotional, verbal, sexual and cyber bullying are ALL an attack!

They are ALL equally damaging. Violence threatens life.

What can administrators, staff and students do to stop it?

Promote a culture of non-violence by writing a script for a video addressing ways to prevent school violence. Consider presenting it to others.

Stadium and Sports Violence

Free speech bombards you with various voices.

Free choice allows you to select your mindset.

Media violence can create a culture where hurting people is glamorized and rewarded.

Promote a culture of non-violence by writing a script for a video addressing ways to stop stadium and sports violence. Consider presenting it to others.

Substance Abuse Can Lead to Violence

At first roses, then perhaps some wine,

a fun time with friends.

How are romance and friendship destroyed?

Promote a culture of non-violence by writing a script for a video addressing ways substance abuse can lead to violence. Consider presenting it to others.

Glamorizing and Normalizing Weapons

Weapons may be highly valued.

How have they become commonplace?

What's the *fallout*?

Promote a culture of non-violence by writing a script for a video addressing ways to stop glamorizing and normalizing weapons. Consider presenting it to others.

Effects of Emotional Violence

Have you heard this? *"Sticks and stones can break my bones but words will never hurt me."* Not true!

What can pierce the heart without penetrating the skin? What can be broken?

Promote a culture of non-violence by writing a script for a video about the effects of emotional violence (bullying, harmful rumors, gossip, prejudice, sexting, name calling, etc.) on victims AND aggressors. Consider presenting it to others.

Anger and Depression Detective

Anger turned inward may become depression.

Depression turned outward may show up as anger.

It helps to uncover what's truly going on.

Identify your hidden feelings.

Create *detective case notes* by completing the sentence starters.

A time I bottled up anger and then felt sad was ____________________

____

____

____

____

I could have expressed my anger safely by ____________________

____

____

____

____

A time I felt sad but expressed it as anger was ____________________

____

____

____

____

What was really bothering me was ____________________

____

____

____

____

Media Violence Diet

Diets suggest giving up goodies.

Yet, healthy and delicious foods can be substituted.

What could be on your *media violence diet* dish?

Promote a culture of non-violence by engaging in a panel discussion about the possibilities of a media violence diet. Prepare for the discussion by writing notes for yourself.

What would you eliminate? ______________________________

What entertainment could take its place? ______________________________

How could it feel to do without aggressive amusement? ______________________________

What could be possible outcomes? ______________________________

Other items you want to bring up: ______________________________

Exceptions to Acceptance

FOR THE FACILITATOR

I. Purpose

Teens actively promote a culture of non-violence.

II. General Comments

Teens are generally encouraged to be open-minded and respect various cultures. The culture of violence is an exception; teens need to discern and refute the subtle and flagrant messages that bombard them. These activities can possibly be presented at elementary, middle and high school programs.

III. Possible Activities

Same Topic for All

Each page may be photocopied and used by all participants for each of nineteen sessions.

Choices

All pages may be photocopied and teens may make individual selections (a different page per several sessions).

Partners or Teams

Teens join peers to complete assigned or chosen pages.

Workshops

The pages can be introduced over several days or weeks.

Committees may work on projects in class or for homework.

The series may culminate in a *Presentation Marathon.*

Panel Discussions and Debates

Teens use the handouts to prepare notes.

Set time limits for each speaker.

Set ground rules that one person speaks at a time, no *put-downs*, no interruptions, etc.

For any of the above formats:

a. Ask a volunteer to read aloud the text in the box at the top of the page.
b. Encourage discussion about the text in the box at the top, the statements and questions.
c. Emphasize that artistic skill, perfect spelling and grammar are not required.
d. Explain that creative ideas and messages that *hit home* are desirable.
e. Allow time for completion.
f. Encourage teens to share their work and to receive peer feedback.

IV. Enrichment Activities

Prompt teens to identify other pop culture messages they want to refute and use similar methods to promote positive ideas (posters, bumper stickers, essays, videos, etc.).

Possibilities

- Body image bias
- Prejudice toward any culture
- Social exclusion

AVOIDING STEREOTYPES AND PREJUDICE 6

The tears of the red, yellow, black, brown and white man are all the same.
~ Martin H. Fischer

Stereotype X or O?

Females are not good enough for team sports.	Racial or ethnic group members all behave alike.	Diversity celebrates differences.
Popular people have better friends.	People in the in-group are more special.	Not all teens are rebellious.
Stereotyping is dangerous	Someone's race does not define the person.	Cultural traditions are worth saving.

It's all about *us* and *them*.	Good looking people are always successful.	Prejudice is an attitude that hurts others.
Rich people are more important than others.	Different groups need to be able to get along.	Certain ethnic groups are smarter than others.
Other people do not need to dictate our attitudes.	Unemployed people have no skills.	Particular religious groups are all terrorists.

Generalizing about any cultural group is wrong.	It's best to avoid all people of certain races.	All members of certain religions are hypocrites.
Snap judgments are usually mistaken.	I can achieve despite what others might think.	A person's sexual orientation matters.
People from different groups can be friends.	People whose beliefs differ from mine are all wrong.	All people deserve a chance.

Minorities are as deserving as majorities.	Macho males do not express feelings.	Some cultures have nice people, but some don't.
The "perfect" body equals a successful person.	We can learn not to judge others.	People's body types are their own fault.
Rich people are selfish.	People not in a clique are not worthy people.	All people deserve respect and rights.

Men and women doing the same job deserve equal pay.	People with disabilities are not very bright.	It is reasonable to have biases against gays and lesbians.
People with differences can work together.	Getting to know individuals decreases stereotyping.	All religious people are judgmental.
Prejudice can be reversed or unlearned.	All people with mental illness are dangerous.	People can rise above bigotry.

It is important to have empathy for targets of prejudice.	People who want sex-change operations are wrong.	All expectations of ethnic or racial groups are correct.
Males are better in math and science.	People from diverse groups can still be like-minded.	Gender, race, ethnicity or sexual orientation should hold people back from being friends.
All people who are disabled want sympathy.	A person who is an only child is always spoiled.	Movies and songs often promote stereotypes.

People who look different ARE different.	People should stick with their own kind.	Different perspectives may lead to creative ideas.
Authority figures are all bossy and strict.	People in the same group can have individual differences.	Low income people are uneducated.
People can and do change.	Certain races or ethnic groups do poorly in some sports.	People in unpopular groups are losers.

Stereotype X or O? – Answer Key

Bold text boxes (open-mindedness) show winning rows.
Boxes not bold (xenophobic) have no winning rows.

Females are not good enough for team sports.	Racial or ethnic group members all behave alike.	**Diversity celebrates differences.**
Popular people have better friends.	People in the in-group are more special.	**Not all teens are rebellious.**
Stereotyping is dangerous	**Someone's race does not define the person.**	**Cultural traditions are worth saving.**

It's all about *us* and *them*.	Good looking people are always successful.	**Prejudice is an attitude that hurts others.**
Rich people are more important than others.	**Different groups need to be able to get along.**	Certain ethnic groups are smarter than others.
Other people do not need to dictate our attitudes.	Unemployed people have no skills.	Particular religious groups are all terrorists.

Generalizing about any cultural group is wrong.	It's best to avoid all people of certain races.	All members of certain religions are hypocrites.
Snap judgments are usually mistaken.	**I can achieve despite what others might think.**	A person's sexual orientation matters.
People from different groups can be friends.	People whose beliefs differ from mine are all wrong.	**All people deserve a chance.**

Minorities are as deserving as majorities.	Macho males do not express feelings.	Some cultures have nice people, but some don't.
The "perfect" body equals a successful person.	**We can learn not to judge others.**	People's body types are their own fault.
Rich people are selfish.	People not in a clique are not worthy people.	**All people deserve respect and rights.**

Men and women doing the same job deserve equal pay.	People with disabilities are not very bright.	It is reasonable to have biases against gays and lesbians.
People with differences can work together.	**Getting to know individuals decreases stereotyping.**	All religious people are judgmental.
Prejudice can be reversed or unlearned.	All people with mental illness are dangerous.	**People can rise above bigotry.**

It is important to have empathy for targets of prejudice.	People who want sex-change operations are wrong.	All expectations of ethnic or racial groups are correct.
Males are better in math and science.	**People from diverse groups can still be like-minded.**	Gender, race, ethnicity or sexual orientation should hold people back from being friends.
All people who are disabled want sympathy.	A person who is an only child is always spoiled.	**Movies and songs often promote stereotypes.**

People who look different ARE different.	People should stick with their own kind.	**Different perspectives may lead to creative ideas.**
Authority figures are all bossy and strict.	**People in the same group can have individual differences.**	Low income people are uneducated.
People can and do change.	Certain races or ethnic groups do poorly in some sports.	People in unpopular groups are losers.

Stereotype – End Exclusion and Embrace Diversity

To exclude means to keep out. Diversity welcomes differences.
Think about words and phrases that relate to these concepts and write them next to the letters.

Example: ***E****mpathy (have empathy and consider how it feels to be excluded)*

E ______________________________

X ______________________________

C ______________________________

L ______________________________

U ______________________________

S ______________________________

I ______________________________

O ______________________________

N ______________________________

D ______________________________

I ______________________________

V ______________________________

E ______________________________

R ______________________________

S ______________________________

I ______________________________

T ______________________________

Y ______________________________

Stereotype X or O?

FOR THE FACILITATOR

I. Purpose

To diminish stereotypes, prejudice and discrimination.

II. General Comments

False ideas about age, ethnic or racial groups, religions, disability, differences, sexual orientation, etc., interfere with social connections, emotional well-being, educational and economic progress.

III. Possible Activities

a. Before session photocopy enough of the *Stereotype – X or O?* handout, page 103, for each teen to have one Tic Tac Toe board; the handout provides enough for seven different game boards.

b. Cut on the broken lines; because there are seven different boards per page, photocopy two pages for fourteen boards or three for twenty-one, etc. (There will be duplicates or triplicates for each).

c. At start of session write X and O on the board and ask what game comes to mind (Tic Tac Toe).

d. Write these terms on the board and elicit definitions: Xenophobia (racism and dislike or fear of foreigners), Stereotype (label), Prejudice (prejudgment) and Discrimination (unfair treatment).

e. Encourage teens to share their experiences as observers or as victims of negative bias.

f. Explain and write on the board that X means Xenophobic and O means Open-Minded.

g. Distribute a Tic Tac Toe cut-out to each teen.

h. Instruct teens to read each box and place an X if the statement is wrong and an O if it's okay.

i. Tell teens that the correct answers result in one or more rows of O's (across, down or diagonally).

j. See Answer Key page 104.

k. Allow time for completion. Then ask teens to share their responses and state why statements are xenophobic or open-minded. (If more than seven teens are in group, some will have copies of the same game board and can take turns sharing different statements).

IV. Enrichment Activities

a. Discuss the pain of rejection and the value of embracing differences (for teens and society).

b. Distribute the *End Exclusion and Embrace Diversity* handout (page 105)

c. Allow time for completion; encourage teens to share ideas as a peer lists them on board.
Examples:

Energize (energize thinking by mingling with people from different backgrounds)
X-Out (x-out or cross out discrimination and prejudice)
Contact (contact breaks down barriers between people from different groups)
Look (look for individual traits rather than assuming typical characteristics among group members)
Universality (we're all members of the human race with more similarities than differences)
Stop (stop stereotyping, stop people from excluding peers)
Include (involve rather than ban people)
One (one person can make a difference by encouraging peers to accept rather than reject someone)
Never (never believe that all members of a group have the same characteristics)

Differences (embrace and celebrate differences)
Information (use intelligence to determine if information is believable or bogus)
Value (people from every race, religion, gender, ethnicity, age, sexual orientation, etc. have value)
Education (the more people learn about individuals the less they believe stereotypes)
Rally (rally around and support people who are hurt by discrimination)
Speak-up (speak out against bigotry which will improve and possibly save lives)
Insight (insight helps people recognize and refute negative stereotypes about themselves)
Think (think about ways to open minds and doors for potential outcasts)
You (you can change negative ideas about yourself, your group and/or other people)

Mix and Mingle

Some students mingle only with friends from the same cultures. Commonalities in these cultures may include behavior, values, beliefs, talents, and/or characteristics of a particular group of people and may relate to age, body (shape, size, and weight), disability, ethnicity, family, gender, neighborhood, race, religion, sexual orientation, social subcultures, spiritual, status (financial, cliques, etc.) or other common bonds (sports, teams, groups, etc.) Others also mingle with friends from mixed cultures.

Draw a map of your school's cafeteria's tables.

Place an ***"S"*** on tables where people of only the ***same*** things in common sit together.

Place a ***"D"*** on tables where people of ***different*** cultures sit together.

Put ***your initials*** on the table where you sit.

1. In what other ways do students stick with people like themselves?

2. In what situations are students from various cultures most likely to mix?

3. What are the benefits of friendships with students from different cultures?

4. What can be done to encourage dissimilar students to mix and mingle?

Mix and Mingle

FOR THE FACILITATOR

I. Purpose

To analyze one's school for signs of self-segregation; to encourage multicultural relationships.

II. General Comments

Many culture cliques still exist.

III. Possible Activities

a. Ask teens to open one hand and pretend each outstretched finger is one of their five closest friends.
b. Tell teens to bend fingers down, which represent friends from their own culture.
c. The fingers that remain outstretched represent friends from different cultures.
d. Ask teens what the number of outstretched fingers suggests about their friendships.
e. (4-5 = mixed; 1-2 = mostly the same culture; 3 = almost equal amount).
f. Explain that teens will consider the level of mixing or matching in their school.
g. Distribute the *Mix and Mingle* handout.
h. A volunteer reads the information and directions aloud.
i. If the teens are unfamiliar with the students at all tables, instruct them to draw the ones they know.
j. Allow time for completion.
k. Encourage teens to share their work.

Possibilities

1. Teens may stick with people who have the same things in common on the bus, at extracurricular, sporting and social events, etc.
2. Teens from various cultures may mix in activities that involve interests or community service.
3. Benefits include exposure to different ideas and preparation for diversity in college and career.
4. Teens may suggest possible Mix and Mingle activities to teachers and the administration.
   Examples
   - Institute a Seat Swap Day – teens draw numbers and sit at the designated lunch tables.
   - Make a bulletin board showing examples of exclusivity and diversity in pop culture.
   - Plan assemblies with civil rights speakers, Holocaust survivors and families, and
   - relevant movies.
   - Determine whether cafeteria staff can host ethnic cuisine days; student volunteers decorate the cafeteria and wear the celebrated country's clothing.

l. Emphasize that it is okay to have friends from one's own culture, but to also connect with different people is educational and enjoyable.

IV. Enrichment Activities

a. Encourage teens to mix and mingle during a ten-minute time span.
b. Teens move around the room as at a party, and become acquainted with peers they don't know well.
   - Encourage teens from different racial or ethnic groups to pair up.
   - If there are an uneven number of participants, one set will be a trio instead of a pair.
   - After five minutes partners go to the front of the room and share what they learned about each other.
c. Ask teens to explore *Mix It Up At Lunch Day,* a project of the Southern Poverty Law Center.

You Can't Judge a Book by Its Cover

The phrase, You can't judge a book by Its cover, means that you cannot judge the quality or character of someone or something just by what you see. People who are judgmental are often insecure, have low self-esteem, succumb to peer pressure, are competitive, jealous and/or lack empathy. They have learned these behaviors as they grew up.

This list of words below indicate different aspects about which people become judgmental. Circle them in the word search.

- **Age**
- **Appearance**
- **Clothes**
- **Disability**
- **Ethnicity**
- **Family**
- **Gender**
- **Intelligence**
- **Popularity**
- **Race**
- **Religion**
- **Sexual Orientation**
- **Shape**
- **Size**
- **Social**
- **Spiritual**
- **Status**
- **Success**
- **Voice**
- **Weight**

G	Z	A	P	O	M	A	Q	S	W	E	S	D	F	Z	X	C	R	T	Y
F	E	G	H	S	U	C	C	E	S	S	J	K	S	L	V	B	N	C	A
P	O	N	Y	T	I	K	Z	X	C	A	G	D	P	C	L	O	T	L	E
S	P	O	D	C	I	A	L	U	W	E	I	G	I	T	V	O	W	O	L
E	O	T	H	E	N	I	C	A	P	P	E	A	R	A	N	C	E	T	A
A	P	P	E	A	R	A	N	L	G	T	Y	U	I	J	K	H	I	H	G
B	U	S	I	S	D	B	I	L	I	E	F	A	T	M	I	L	G	E	Y
P	L	R	E	L	I	G	I	O	N	R	A	C	U	S	I	Z	H	S	F
S	A	C	C	E	S	S	S	R	E	X	U	A	A	L	U	W	T	B	L
S	R	I	R	I	A	T	U	I	E	S	T	E	L	L	R	O	U	N	D
S	I	T	A	T	B	S	O	E	R	I	E	S	N	T	P	A	P	L	E
C	T	A	S	G	I	S	I	N	T	E	L	L	I	G	E	N	C	E	S
S	Y	D	T	P	L	I	H	T	L	N	R	A	L	Z	R	H	O	R	T
O	R	F	A	M	I	L	Y	A	I	A	A	D	Y	K	E	L	N	S	A
C	W	J	T	O	T	T	G	T	P	M	C	F	N	A	M	L	M	F	T
I	E	K	U	P	Y	V	O	I	C	E	K	G	N	T	I	M	E	N	U
I	X	E	S	U	I	E	A	O	E	Y	W	I	S	O	C	I	A	L	E
L	O	R	A	L	E	T	H	N	I	C	I	T	Y	H	T	S	N	A	L

On the list above, put a check mark in front of the three words that are most meaningful to you. On the back, explain your reasons for selecting the words.

You Can't Judge a Book by Its Cover

FOR THE FACILITATOR

I. Purpose

To help teens identify motives for judgmental attitudes and encourage teens to look beyond the surface.

II. General Comments

Teens who find fault are encouraged to accept and learn more about people despite differences and appearances.

III. Possible Activities

a. Ask for the definition of *judgmental* (to make unfair conclusions based on limited information).
b. Encourage teens to share times people made unfair judgments about them (responses will be personalized).
c. Encourage teens to brainstorm what motivates people to be judgmental; a peer lists their ideas on the board.
Possibilities
- Disrespecting everyone's right to be different
- Bias, pre-judging before knowing all the facts
- Thinking *"my way is the only way"*
- False superiority and snobbishness
- My family said so
- Guilt
- Hostility
- Hypocrisy

d. Ask "When you put someone down, do you raise yourself up?" (no, you may show your own weakness).
e. Distribute the *You Can't Judge a Book by Its Cover* handout.
f. A volunteer reads the directions at the top and at the bottom of the page.
g. Encourage a brief discussion of the word meanings.
h. Allow time for completion.
i. Encourage teens to share their most meaningful words from the list and reasons for choosing them.
j. Encourage a discussion about sit-coms, comedy acts, song lyrics and conversations that promote put-downs.
k. Discuss role models in teens' lives. Who builds them up or tears them down?
l. Ask teens to examine situations in which they tend to be most critical, with whom and why.
m. Conversely, ask teens to consider when and with whom they are least likely to be judgmental.
n. Ask about how people may feel who are judged (hurt, demoralized).
o. Encourage teens to identify reasons not to judge (they would not want to be judged; they do not have all the facts; people being judged are usually doing the best they can and judgers might do the same in similar situations; and because someone is different does not mean the person is inferior, etc.).
p. Ask teens how to handle being unjustly judged (do not let the judger control or define you).
q. Emphasize that we do not know how we would act if we had the same influences as the persons we criticize; we need to treat others as we want to be treated, with compassion.

IV. Enrichment Activities

a. Encourage a discussion about judging people based on one's own issues e.g. a person who acts dishonestly may call others liars or thieves.
b. Ask teens to analyze the saying *Variety is the spice of life* (differences make relationships interesting).
c. If appropriate for your teens introduce the concept that people who profess to strongly hate a group may have related conflicts.
Example: Teens who bash people who are in same sex relationships may secretly question their own sexual orientation.

Labels Can Come True

Labels pigeonhole people or categorize them without much thought.

Labels People Put On Me ↓	Labels I Put on Myself ↓	Labels I Put On Others ↓

Give an example of someone allowing a negative label to come true.

____

____

Give an example of someone living up to a positive label.

____

____

Labels Can Come True

FOR THE FACILITATOR

I. Purpose
To illustrate the impact of labels on oneself and others.

II. General Comments
Teens may act to perpetuate a negative label or a positive trait.

III. Possible Activities

Optional Opener for the Session

- Before session open a can of tomato sauce, leave a safe edge and empty the contents.
- At the start of session, discuss the nutrition info on the label; do not reveal that the can is empty.
- Pretend to accidentally dump the contents on a nearby teen (nothing will spill out).
- Elicit that labels don't tell everything. Distribute blank labels or sticky notes.
- Ask teens to describe themselves on the labels. Encourage teens to share their own descriptions.

Introduction to the *Labels Can Come True* handout.

a. Display some labels; ask about their purpose (to define something or someone).
b. Ask how teens tend to label groups *(athletes – jocks).*
c. Ask what negative labels they give others or themselves *(stupid).*
d. Elicit examples of positive labels *(smart).*
e. Distribute the handout; allow time for completion.
f. Encourage teens to share their labels (responses may include positive and negative terms).
Example of someone allowing a negative label to come true:
A person states that all teens are rude; a teen makes an obscene gesture which acts out the label, and also validates the person's belief about teens being rude.
Example of someone *living up to* a positive label:
Club members pride themselves in being caring; a teen who belongs to the club volunteers at a hospital.
g. Ask the following questions; possible responses are parenthesized:

- How do people treat a person on whom they have placed a negative label? (as if the label is true)
- What often happens in the labeled person's mind? (person may come to believe the label is true).
- How does a negative label affect the person's feelings? (sadness, anger, feeling left out).
- How does the label affect the person's actions? (often acts as if the label is true).
- What are some examples of acting out one's negative label? (the *loner* may become more i solated, the *outsider* may plot to harm the in-group, etc).
- How could a person put a positive spin on one's own label? (defy a negative label: if called *"stupid,"* display an area of expertise. Celebrate a label that's due to difference: if an ethnic slur, share country's music or food).
- What are the real problems with labels? (labels are lies that can come true).
- What can be said about **labelers**? (they lack critical thinking skills, do not bother to delve into the many aspects of a person, try to build up their own status by tearing people down).
- What about positive labels? (better than negative but any label reduces a complex person to one aspect; people have many qualities worth knowing, not only the one label).

IV. Enrichment Activities
Encourage a discussion of mindsets that stop labeling.

Possibilities

- Delve into diversity – ask, listen and learn rather than automatically disliking the differences.
- Look for similarities among people with superficial dissimilarity.
- Think about ridiculous labels. (a math whiz is called stupid because of poor spelling).
- Powerful negative labels become stigmas; stigmas prevent people from seeking help and have caused teens to harm themselves and others.

Scapegoat Forum

Directions for the Chair Person

Copy the illustration on the right onto the board and point to it.
Ask questions in bold type and call on volunteers to respond.
There are no right or wrong answers.
Possibilities are parenthesized or bulleted.
Do NOT read responses aloud until after participants speak.

1. **How did the package wind up on the animal?** (someone placed it there).
2. **Who owned the *Loser* package originally?** (the person who placed it there).
3. **Why did the person place it on the animal?** (they wanted to get rid of it).
4. **Who is the real loser?** (the person who displaced their garbage onto the innocent animal).
5. **What is a scapegoat?** (a person or group who is blamed).
6. **What *burdens* are placed on human scapegoats?** (guilt, aggression, insecurity, fear, ignorance).
7. **What's in it for the scapegoaters?** (false superiority, false relief).
8. **Name places where scapegoating occurs** (playgrounds, schools, families, teams).
9. **What are examples of the following types of scapegoating?**
   - **Person against person** (a worker blames another for lost business).
   - **Many against one** (team members blame one player for a loss).
   - **Group against group** (a clique against outsiders).
   - **A majority against a minority** (ethnic, racial, religious, sexual orientation, disability, etc.).
   - **One against a group** (a bomber blames the masses for personal misery).
10. **Recall a situation when you were the scapegoater.** (answers will be individualized).
11. **Recall a situation when you were the scapegoat.** (answers will be individualized).
12. **Give examples of people blaming the youth culture for society's problems.**
    - Sexual promiscuity
    - Violence
    - Alcohol and drug abuse
    - Abortions
    - Out of wedlock births
    - Vulgar lyrics
    - Academic deficiencies
13. **What can scapegoated individuals or groups do to empower themselves?**
    - Report scapegoating to school staff or appropriate officials.
    - Speak respectfully in defense of self or the group.
    - Write letters to editors and/or articles for school newspapers and other publications.
    - Contact public or political officials for assistance and publicity.
    - Communicate in a positive manner on social media, respectfully advocating for self or others.
    - Act as a positive role model if you belong to a group that is negatively labeled.
    - Align with advocacy groups.
    - Develop support systems (friends, family).
14. **How can you be an ally to a scapegoated individual or group?**
    - Speak up in favor of them.
    - Speak out against scapegoating.
    - Advocate through the written word (in print and electronically).
    - Be a friend.

Scapegoat Forum

FOR THE FACILITATOR

I. Purpose

To recognize that scapegoaters displace their own negativity onto other individuals and/or groups.

To identify ways to empower scapegoats (people who are made to take the blame for others).

II. General Comments

Teens view an illustration then respond to questions in a forum format.

Teens will be less likely to scapegoat others when they recognize that it reveals their own insecurities.

III. Possible Activities

a. Before session recruit a volunteer who has a strong back to be positioned on hands and knees.
b. When session starts the volunteer assumes the position, simulating an animal on four legs.
c. Ask another volunteer to place a few books on the person's back.
d. Ask teens what is being demonstrated (placing a burden on a person or an animal).
e. The volunteers sit and the audience claps.
f. Write *Scapegoat* on the board and ask its meaning (a person or group who is blamed).
g. Explain that teens will play forum speakers and respond to the chairperson's questions.
h. Ask for a volunteer who is comfortable drawing an illustration on the board and reading aloud.
i. Provide the volunteer chairperson with the *Scapegoat Forum* handout.
j. The chairperson is positioned at the front of the room or the head of the table.
k. The chairperson draws the illustration on the board and reads the questions.
l. Reinforce that people may volunteer to speak; no one will be *put on the spot.*
m. The chairperson calls on people whose hands are raised.
n. After the questions are answered, all clap for the chairperson.
o. Ask teens the most important concept they learned from the session (answers will vary).
p. Emphasize that the *package, burden, rubbish* (negativity) belongs to the **scapegoat-er**.

IV. Enrichment Activities

a. Ask teens to create posters about scapegoating.
b. Remind teens that artistic skill or perfect grammar and spelling are not required.
c. Prompt teens to use their imaginations and creativity.
d. Encourage teens to share their posters.
e. If feasible, post their work in a prominent location.

More Than Meets the Eye

Rank from 1-10 people I now admire	The Present	The Future	Rank from 1-10 people I might admire
# ______	16 year old who stutters severely	Wins verdicts as a famous trial lawyer	# ______
# ______	Star high school athlete	Is physically injured during a fight	# ______
# ______	Most popular	Is part of an abusive relationship	# ______
# ______	A heavy person is not accepted for a dance solo in high school	Wins National television dance contest	# ______
# ______	Class valedictorian	Fries brain on drugs	# ______
# ______	Snickered at due to facial scars	Is a plastic surgeon for burn victims	# ______
# ______	Received new sports car for graduation	Caused an accident driving drunk	# ______
# ______	Bullied because of accent	Is an interpreter at the United Nations	# ______
# ______	Tormented by racial slurs	Is a respected civil rights activist	# ______
# ______	A homeless 15-year-old runaway	Runs a rehab for troubled teens	# ______
# ______	Wins a million dollars	Declares bankruptcy	# ______

More Than Meets the Eye

FOR THE FACILITATOR

I. Purpose
To acknowledge that stereotypical assumptions are often untrue and that people can change.

II. General comments
Teens will see that the appearance of fame or failure doesn't always predict the future.

III. Possible Activities

a. Before session photocopy the *More than Meets the Eye* handouts; cut box and the down the middle on the dashed lines.

b. Teens will initially see only *The Present.*

c. Write *Looks are deceiving* on the board and ask teens to share situations when this was true for them.

d. Distribute the left half of the cut out box *(The Present)* of the *More than Meets the Eye* handout.

e. Explain that teens will read descriptions and rank order them in the first column.

f. The scale is #1, most admired - #10, least admired.

g. Allow time for completion.

h. Encourage teens to share responses and reasons.

i. Ask teens to turn *The Present* half over.

j. Distribute the right side of the handout and ask teens to read *The Future* portion of each person's life and ask them to rank order again, based on new knowledge about the person.

k. Allow time for completion.

l. Encourage teens to share responses and reasons.

m. Allow teens to put the two halves together and notice their rankings of the same person, in different times of their lives.

n. Ask teens what was illustrated by the activity (in addition to the inability to foretell the future).

o. Elicit the italicized concepts.

Ask

- What negative stereotypes were assumed about some of the teens? *speech problems or scars prevent success, people are at a disadvantage if English is their second language, members of racial minorities are unfortunate, homeless runaways are doomed to fail.*
- What glowing generalizations were made about the positive attributes? *physical strength, popularity, brains and money mean success.*
- Was luck responsible for what happened to the people in the future? *no*
- What was the main contributor to each person's future? *personal choices – to attend law school, to fight, to remain in a dysfunctional relationship, to dance despite body build, to use drugs, to use expertise to help others, to drink and drive, to use skills for a career, to advocate for equality, to help troubled teens, to be reckless with wealth.*
- When you look at a person's present circumstances, what can't you see? *their unique traits*
- What qualities helped the teens have better futures? *Motivation, determination, compassion, etc.*

IV. Enrichment Activities
Encourage insight by asking teens to share personal experiences:

- Times they were stereotyped – how it felt, whether it was true and the outcome.
- Times they stereotyped a person – how they think the person felt and how they will stop stereotyping.

Mob Mentality or Me?

MOB MENTALITY

ME

Two people beat each other up and everyone cheers them on.	My friends bully someone.	Everyone says any student who failed the test is stupid.	My best friends say people from an ethnic group are all alike.	Several friends at a party talk against a race of people.
People on my team trash a player's sexual orientation.	Everyone walks past someone who fell.	My partner's parents say women should be stay-at-home moms.	My friends make fun of a person's accent.	A person I want to date mimics someone's limp.
My friends laugh about someone's speech impediment.	My clique puts down people who can't afford things.	People in my phys. ed. class stare at over or underweight students.	Customers in line with me shove to get the new phone.	My friends say all people from a certain country are terrorists.
My friends won't allow anyone who has an unusual body size into our study group.	My family wants me to date only within my own race or ethnic group.	My friends make fun of others' religious customs.	My partner's friends are rude to someone who wants to change gender.	My family says my aspirations are not appropriate for my gender.
My friends will no longer accept me if I walk in a Pride parade.	My friends laughed hysterically at a sign language interpreter.	My friends pressure me to spread rumors about someone they dislike.	My friends tell me to avoid a student who is HIV+.	My partner's family makes racial or ethnic slurs.

Mob Mentality or Me?

FOR THE FACILITATOR

I. Purpose

To illustrate examples of mob mentality and motivate teens to make individual decisions.

II. General Comments

Teens who want acceptance may be tempted to follow the crowd and contribute to prejudice or violence.

III. Possible Activities

a. Before session cut the *Mob Mentality or Me?* handout on the broken lines and procure tape to post the signs; cut the bottom portion of the handout into squares and place cutouts face down.
b. Ask teens to raise hands if they have yelled and sang loudly at a game or concert (most will).
c. Ask how many would yell and sing if they were the only one doing it (few would).
d. Write *Mob Mentality* on the board and ask its meaning (people tend to act like others in a group).
e. Ask teens to brainstorm examples as a volunteer lists them on the board.
   Possibilities
   - People flock to a crowded restaurant assuming the food must be good.
   - Fans destroy property after their team lost a game.
   - War criminals say they were *just following orders*.
   - Salem witch trials took place when a town ganged up on innocent people.
   - Jonestown, Guyana where people drank poison in a mass suicide to follow their leader.
   - Bystanders do nothing as people get hurt.
f. Encourage a discussion of related concepts.
   In a group:
   - People often lose their individuality and/or their sense of self-awareness.
   - People are less likely to refrain from wrongdoing thinking they will not be singled out and caught.
   - People feel less personal responsibility.
   - People who identify blindly with a group are more likely to give in to peer pressure.
g. Place the *MOB MENTALITY* sign on one wall and the *ME* sign on the opposite wall.
h. Explain that volunteers will take turns reading a cutout statement aloud.
i. Peers will then move to one side of the room or the other side depending on which sign applies.
j. Ask teens to dig deep and think honestly about what they would do in the situations.
k. Teens will stand under the *MOB MENTALITY* sign if they would go along with the crowd.
l. Emphasize that bystanders who would do nothing belong under the *MOB MENTALITY* sign.
m. Peers will stand under the *ME* sign if they would act differently to right a wrong.
n. Teens under the *MOB MENTALITY* sign explain why they would *go with the flow.*
o. Teens under the *ME* sign share their specific actions, e.g., *I would help the person who fell.*
p. Teens under the *ME* sign share what they would say, e.g., *People in any ethnic group are unique individuals.*
q. Regardless of what they might actually do, many teens will probably stand under the *ME* sign.
r. By stating how they would respond they reinforce the likelihood of acting as caring individuals.
s. If many stand under the *ME* sign there becomes peer pressure to act in a responsible way.
t. If only a few stand under the *ME* sign, point out there might be peer pressure to conform.

IV. Enrichment Activities

a. Encourage teens to share examples of mob mentality they have witnessed.
b. Ask teens to share information about times they did things as part of a group that they would not ordinarily do.
c. Ask teens to share stories about times they advocated for victims of prejudice and the outcome.

Join Hands

Hand-dominance is mostly developed before birth.
Lefties today are not blamed or bullied for being different.
Yet, people with other inborn traits are often discriminated against.

Label each hand with a primarily inborn trait that people criticize.

How can you reach out to someone you know who has one of the traits?

How can you encourage people you know to *join hands* despite differences?

Join Hands

FOR THE FACILITATOR

I. Purpose

To recognize that most prejudice is directed toward traits that are determined before birth.

II. General Comments

Teens will be less likely to blame or bully people whose differences are due to human nature.

III. Possible Activities

a. Ask teens who are left-handed to stand.

b. Ask peers if they realized these people were left-handed.

c. Discuss that years ago parents tried to force their children to be right-handed even though they were left-hand dominant.

d. Discuss that some differences are hidden (e.g. hand dominance) but some seem more noticeable.

e. Distribute the *Join Hands* handout and ask a volunteer to read the information in the box aloud.

f. Allow time for completion.

g. Encourage teens to share their responses.

Possibilities

Traits with possible biological influences that people criticize (some of these might be controversial):

- Height, weight, body build
- Facial features
- The need for eyeglasses and/or braces
- Several disabilities (exceptions are those resulting from accidents or diseases later in life, etc.)
- Race and ethnicity
- Gender
- The lightness or darkness of skin within a race of people with brown or black skin
- Religion is not inborn but may be determined by parents before birth and until a child is old enough to choose.
- Sexual orientation
- Gender identity

Teens can reach out to someone with one of the traits in several ways:

- Start a conversation
- Exchange cell phone numbers, etc.
- Invite the person to eat lunch with them
- Plan an activity with the person
- Ask about customs

Teens can encourage people with differences to join in several ways:

- Including diverse people in friendship circles, lunch table, clubs and activities
- Advocating for people with disabilities or other differences
- Working with peers and school staff on programs to promote diversity (ethnic costume contests, having peers from other countries teach some conversational phrases to English speaking students)

IV. Enrichment Activities

a. Encourage teens to plan a multicultural party (for as many ethnic and racial groups as possible) with the following committees: Ethnic Edibles, Music and Dance, Decorations, Games and Recreation, etc.

b. If possible, actually have the party!

My Roots

Your *roots* stem from people who influence you
and from places and things that have special meaning to you.

Express yourself by creating a quatrain in each box below.
(A quatrain is a four line stanza or poem with any rhyme pattern.)

If you wish, add or substitute a drawn picture.

My Person

My Place

A Thing

My Roots

FOR THE FACILITATOR

I. Purpose

To consider roots (cultural origins) as persons, places and things that influenced and helped teens form ideas about life.

II. General Comments

Attitudes toward people and groups, prejudice or acceptance, usually develop early.

III. Possible Activities

a. Write *Roots* on the board and ask its meaning (in this context, cultural origins). Elicit aspects of one's *roots*:

- ancestors, family, first friends, parental occupations, etc.
- stories told by older generations
- native country, foods, music, dance
- traditions
- toys from childhood, places children played

b. Explain that teens will create quatrains, four line poems with any rhyme pattern. Additionally or alternatively they may depict a person, place and thing that impacted them.

c. You may put the examples on the board.

Example of a quatrain about a **person**.

My Dad

Live and let live.
Walk a mile in their shoes.
Pearls of wisdom he'd give
And expect me to use.

Example of a quatrain about a **place:**

My Home Away from Home

Walls of green,
So serene.
Aunt's apartment though small.
Was my all and all.

Example of a quatrain about a **thing***:*

The Recovery Book

It was hidden under the table;
He read it each day on the sly.
When old enough to be able,
I asked of the secrecy – *Why?*

d. Distribute the *My Roots* handout.

- Ask for examples of parent/caregivers' messages (hatred, prejudice, acceptance, etc.).
- Encourage contemplation about a person who influenced their views about people or groups.
- Encourage contemplation about places that impacted teens positively or negatively.
- Encourage contemplation about objects that affected teens' attitudes.
- Allow time for completion.
- Encourage teens to share their poems and receive peer feedback.

IV. Enrichment Activities

a. Encourage teens to explore the poem *Where I'm From* by George Ella Lyon available on her website. Note that this poem is not in quatrains and does not rhyme.

b. Ask teens to write and share poems in a similar format.

Dr. Martin Luther King, Jr.'s Wisdom

Light and Love

"Darkness cannot drive out darkness; only light can do that.
Hate cannot drive out hate; only love can do that."

~ **Dr. Martin Luther King, Jr.**

Dr. Martin Luther King, Jr.'s Wisdom

FOR THE FACILITATOR

I. Purpose

To apply Dr. Martin Luther King, Jr.'s civil rights quotations to today's issues concerning any marginalized group.

II. General Comments

Teens use their imaginations to depict concepts that affect their lives.

III. Possible Activities

a. Ask teens to recall information about Dr. Martin Luther King, Jr.
Elicit that he was a major civil rights activist, achieved a doctorate degree, received the Nobel Peace Prize and other honors and was assassinated.

b. Explain that teens will apply his wisdom to situations faced today regarding all types of discrimination.

c. Distribute the *Dr. Martin Luther King, Jr.'s Wisdom* handout.

d. Ask a volunteer to read the quotation aloud.

e. Explain that teens will depict and/or describe their interpretations of the quotation.

f. Teens may sketch, make cartoons or caricatures, use symbols, and/or write prose, poetry or lyrics, about the quotation.

g. Remind teens not to worry about artistic skills, spelling and grammar when preparing this response; self-expression and content is most important.

h. Allow time for completion.

i. Encourage teens to share their work and receive peer feedback.

j. Write the quotations below on the board (one at a time) and prompt teens to apply them to their lives. Alternatively, present these other MLK quotes in subsequent sessions; teens depict and/or describe their interpretations.

- "We must learn to live together as brothers or perish together as fools."
- "Hate destroys the hater."
- "Let no man pull you so low as to hate him."
- "Our lives begin to end the day we become silent about things that matter."

IV. Enrichment Activities

a. Ask a volunteer to list the following bolded names on the board:

- **Sojourner Truth** – spoke against slavery and the death penalty; promoted women's rights.
- **Harriet Beecher Stowe** – helped slaves escape as part of the Underground Railroad.
- **Cesar Chavez** – helped improve conditions for farm workers.
- **Margaret Sanger** – was a birth control advocate, sex educator and nurse.
- **Susan B. Anthony** – advocated for women's suffrage (the right to vote).
- **Ryan White** – was a teen with HIV; became an activist for research and anti-discrimination.
- **Dr. Jacobus Ten Broek** – Founded American Federation of the Blind; promoted white canes.

b. Ask if anyone is familiar with these people and to tell the group what they know about them.

c. If they are not familiar with any of these names, share the information after each name above.

d. Encourage teens to research quotations and biographical data about these and others who promoted respect for others and equality of opportunities.

ADVOCACY IN ACTION 7

We must always take sides.
Neutrality helps the oppressor, never the victim.
Silence encourages the tormenter, never the tormented.
~ Elie Wiesel

The Difference One Person Can Make

United States President Barack Obama reminds us regarding Nelson Mandela:
"... to forward the example that he set: ...
to never discount the difference that one person can make..."

From his childhood as a herd boy, Nelson Mandela went on to lead the African National Congress' struggle against South Africa's racially oppressive apartheid regime. For his efforts, he spent 27 years behind bars as a political prisoner. He was later awarded the Nobel Peace Prize and became the first South African president who was Black.

- *Apartheid* in South Africa was racial segregation; political, economic and legal discrimination; privileges were granted to people of European origin.
- *Social apartheid* is segregation based on status – an *underclass* is excluded from the mainstream.

Put your own spin on *apartheid* by noting examples in the three boxes below.

Similarities to Apartheid at My School

Types of Separation	**People of Privilege**	**The *Underclassed***

"What counts in life is not the mere fact that we have lived. It is what difference we have made to the lives of others that will determine the significance of the life we lead."

~ From *Nelson Mandela By Himself: The Authorised Book of Quotations*

I, one person, can make a positive difference in the lives of others at my school by...

____

____

____

Other students may follow my example by ...

____

____

____

The Difference One Person Can Make

FOR THE FACILITATOR

I. Purpose

To use Nelson Mandela's example to fight against types of separation, privilege and underclass exclusion that occur in **some** schools today.

II. General Comments

Teens apply the political concept of apartheid (racial segregation) to their social environment and empower themselves to change it.

III. Possible Activities

a. Write *South Africa in the past and our school today* on the board.

b. Ask teens about the connection (teens may be aware that social inequalities existed in South Africa in the past and possibly at school today).

c. Distribute the *The Difference One Person Can Make* handout.

d. Ask a volunteer to read the text including the directions above the diagram aloud.

e. Explain that *underclass* does not mean *underclassmen* (students not yet seniors) but refers those who are treated as *underdogs.*

f. Allow time for individual completion of the page, or draw diagram on the board and ask teens to brainstorm as a peer writes their ideas on the diagram.

Possibilities

- **Types of Separation:** may be based on age (freshmen ... seniors), body build and/or appearance, disability, ethnicity, family, race, religion, social or economic status, sexual orientation, spirituality. Other examples include academics, athletics, extracurricular activities, interests, etc.
- **People of Privilege:** may be those who are labeled as smart, popular, jocks, and cheerleaders, student council officers, financially well-off, etc. Privilege and power may be obtained through intimidation e.g. cliques who bully or exclude.
- **Examples of Underclass:** any individual or group that is excluded, made fun of or bullied usually due to looking or acting differently, being new, experiencing academic challenges, having a disability, etc.

g. If the diagram was completed as a group project, allow time for each teen to complete the rest of the page independently.

h. Encourage teens to share what they, as individuals, can do to make a positive difference in the lives of others at their school.

Examples

- Include those who are separated e.g., sit at lunch with someone who is new, has a different sexual orientation, looks different, has a disability, etc.
- Ask administrators to help set up an *Abolish Social Apartheid* program at school.

i. Encourage teens to share how others may follow their example.

Possibilities

- One person sits with an excluded person and others join them.
- Students perceived as leaders include the formerly labeled *underclassed* and peers follow.

IV. Enrichment Activities

Motivate teens to research other aspects of Nelson Mandela's life, e.g., how after he was released from prison he forgave those who imprisoned him.

Open Mic Dialogue

Prepare for your turn at the microphone.
Write one prejudicial situation and one possible solution for each category.
Then share your thoughts and ask for audience opinions.

SITUATION	POSSIBLE SOLUTIONS
Home	**Home**
Neighborhood	**Neighborhood**
School	**School**

Open Mic Dialogue

FOR THE FACILITATOR

I. Purpose

To consider ways to advocate in prejudicial situations close to home.

II. General Comments

Teens will use the open mic format to stimulate anti-discrimination discussions.

III. Possible activities

a. If available obtain a podium (or table) and microphone (or empty water bottle).

b. Ask the definition of open mic nights (live shows where audience members may perform at the microphone).

c. Point out that open mic nights usually involve comedy, music, poetry, etc. but this open mic event is an opportunity to speak their minds about anti-discrimination.

d. Model the role of an open mic dialogue initiator for teens by using the props and asking the following questions; encourage audience to give their opinions; possible responses are parenthesized:

- The situation is at home – your parents/caregivers forbid inter-racial dating and you really like the person. What are some possible positive solutions? (Ask an open-minded adult to talk with them.)
- The situation is in your neighborhood – neighbors say that newcomers look like terrorists. What are some possible positive solutions? (Tell neighbors: *Terrorists can look like you and me.*)
- The situation is at school – students joke about someone's weight. What are some possible positive solutions? (Tell peers: *It's the size of the heart that matters.)*

e. Distribute the *Open Mic Dialogue* handout; a volunteer reads the directions aloud.

Team Option

- Divide the group into three teams, Home, Neighborhood and School.
- Each team elects a writer to record their ideas.
- Teams brainstorm a few situations and possible solutions for their categories.
- The group re-convenes and teammates take turns sharing their responses at the mic.
- The audience provides opinions.

Individual Option

- Individuals complete the handout writing one situation and possible solution for each category.
- Teens take turns sharing their responses at the mic.
- The audience provides opinions.

Possibilities

SITUATION	POSSIBLE SOLUTION
Home	**Home**
Parents/caregivers don't want teens to have friends from certain cultures.	Remind caregivers about people from those cultures who contributed to the arts, science, etc.
Neighborhood	**Neighborhood**
Discriminatory graffiti sends the wrong message in your community.	Gather friends and ask officials if you can clean the graffiti and create a pro-diversity message.
School	**School**
You overhear crude comments about different cultures.	Write an article in the school newspaper about embracing diversity.

IV. Enrichment Activities

Continue the open mic theme for the next session. Encourage teens to compose songs, poetry or skits that promote diversity, and then perform for peers.

Outrage-Us

A human rights violation that I think is outrageous is ____

____

____

____

____

____ .

"I am only one, but still I am one. I cannot do everything, but still I can do something;

~ Helen Keller

Something I can do is ____

____

____

____

____ .

"There is also strength in numbers.
The more individuals or organizations
that you can rally towards your cause, the better."

~ Mark Shields

I can team up with ____

____

____

____

____ .

We will be a powerful positive force by ____

____

____

____

____

____ .

Outrage-Us

FOR THE FACILITATOR

I. Purpose

To instill productive outrage and positive individual action; to influence peers to advocate for equality.

II. General Comments

To embrace diversity entails personal and group responsibility to help people who are oppressed.

III. Possible Activities

a. Write *Outrageous* on the board and ask its meaning (shockingly violating acceptable standards).

b. Distribute the *Outrage-Us* handout; a volunteer reads the two quotations aloud.

c. Ask teens about Helen Keller (overcame loss of sight and hearing; a leading humanitarian).

d. Ask about Mark Shields (a political columnist and commentator).

e. Ideally teens will contemplate human rights violations and identify their outrages. Alternatively ask teens to brainstorm human rights violations and list them on the board.

f. The Bigotry Bank below may be copied onto the board if your teens need these prompts

Bigotry Bank

Hate Crimes and Hate Groups	Discrimination Against People With Disabilities	Ageism Directed Toward Teens Or Elders	Prejudice Or Preferential Treatment Due To Looks	Discrimination Based On Sexual Orientation
Gender Bias Or Harassment	Socioeconomic Status Stereotypes	Educational Inequalities	Racism Or Ethnic Discrimination	Religious Intolerance

g. Encourage teens to share their responses.

h. Examples of individual actions teens can take:
- Speak and write about damage done by racial slurs and ethnic or other prejudicial jokes.
- Refute myths and stereotypes.
- Research biographies of leaders in immigration, equal education for girls in developing countries, etc.
- Take pride in their own heritage by inviting friends from other cultures to their homes.

i. Teens can team up with others:
- Initiate a Diversity Club.
- Obtain permission from administration to organize teens from different cultures to share their customs and challenges in assemblies.
- Approach band and chorus leaders about including music from many cultures.
- Visit each other's spiritual services to learn more about different faiths.
- Work together on a collage of ads and photos that promote multicultural inclusion.
- Host fundraisers and donate proceeds to an anti-discrimination organization.

j. Encourage teens to research groups that promote diversity.

Possibilities
- The Anti-Defamation League
- The Southern Poverty Law Center

IV. Enrichment Activities

Encourage teens to explore exploitation of vulnerable populations:
- Human trafficking including sexual slavery and forced labor.
- Child labor, child soldiers and teen sweatshops.
- Wrongful arrests, imprisonment based on racial or ethnic profiling.

Do I Have It In Me?

Unscramble the words below that describe people who embrace diversity.

__________________ npoe-mnided . . . (receptive to new ideas)
__________________ rfnielyd . . . . (favorable toward people)
__________________ tisevines. . . . . . . (sympathetic to others' feelings)
__________________ esrctpeluf . . . . . . (attitude of admiration)
__________________ avrbe . . . . (courageous)
__________________ arcngi . . . . (compassionate)
__________________ nkdi . . . . (thoughtful)
__________________ nilcusvie . . . . (not excluding any person or group)
__________________ daovacet . . . . . . (speak up in favor of someone or something)
__________________ leerad. . . . . (guide others)
__________________ other
__________________ other

Write the traits that best describe you on the lines below.

Me

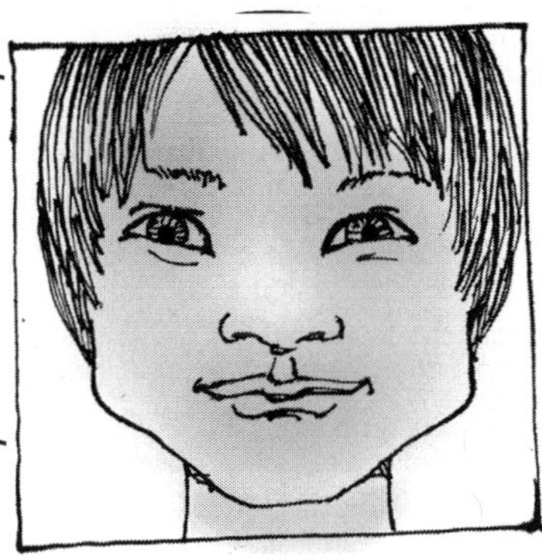

What trait do you value the most? ________________________________

How can you use that trait to support people who experience discrimination? ________________

____

Do I Have It In Me?

FOR THE FACILITATOR

I. Purpose

To adopt qualities that promote advocacy for people who experience discrimination.

II. General Concepts

A word scramble puzzle reinforces traits of people who embrace diversity.

III. Possible Activities

a. Write on the board *Do I have it in me to …* and ask volunteers to complete the sentence.

b. Responses will vary e.g. *to ask someone out, to win the game, to graduate, to be loyal*, etc.

c. Explain that qualities within people help them understand and stick up for people.

d. Ask teens to brainstorm traits; a volunteer lists their ideas on the board (accept reasonable traits).

e. Distribute the *Do I Have It In Me?* handout and allow time for completion.

f. Encourage teens to share their word scramble solutions.

Answer Key

- Open-minded
- Friendly
- Sensitive
- Respectful
- Brave
- Caring
- Kind
- Inclusive
- Advocate
- Leader
- Other (responses will vary)

g. Ask teens to share their responses to the questions below the illustration (answers will be individualized).

h. Encourage a discussion about traits of an advocate.

Possibilities

- Willingness to express a potentially unpopular opinion.
- Courage to stand up for people.
- A positive attitude toward the people being helped.
- A belief that others can change their prejudicial attitudes.

i. Ask teens to discuss leadership qualities.

Possibilities

- Willingness to join an anti-discrimination group, charity or other organization.
- Ability to move outside one's comfort zone.
- Responsibility to complete assigned tasks.
- Initiative to see what needs to be done and help others do it.
- Creativity to find ways to reach people (those who need advocacy and those who are prejudiced).
- Enthusiasm to inspire people to fight non-violently for a cause.

IV. Enrichment Activities

Encourage a discussion of the qualities needed by people who experience discrimination. These may include belief in self despite degrading remarks, innuendos or being ignored by others; bravery to speak up for oneself to bullies and to tell people in authority; faith that a system, society and individuals can change, etc.

Giving Back

What can you do to give back to the universe?

Rate your level of interest on the following:

1 - GREAT IDEA **2 - WILL CONSIDER** **3 - NOT FOR ME**

___With a choir, or group of musicians, or solo, call hospitals or skilled care facilities, and offer your talents.

___Tutor young children who are in hospitals or confined at home, on subjects in which you specialize.

___Help older adults manage their "modern-day" technical issues (cell phone, computer, notepad, etc.)

___Create a web page or social media page for a local non-profit.

___Sign up for donor donations.

___Give blood to the Red Cross when of age.

___Collect canned goods in the neighborhood and donate to the local food bank, AIDs homes, etc.

___Organize volunteers to pick up papers/garbage strewn along the road or in public parks.

___Offer to work in a soup kitchen.

___Re-gift something you received to someone who needs it more than you.

___Organize a book and/or toy drive for a local shelter or children's clinic.

___Clean your closet and donate clothes you don't wear to an organization that helps homeless teens or battered partners.

___Play games at a local senior citizen center with the seniors.

___Host a Diaper Drive and or a Personal Products Drive (shampoo, soap, toothpaste, shaving cream, razors, toothbrush) for area shelters.

___Collect PG and G-rated movies that you and others no longer watch and then donate them to a local children's hospital or pediatric floor of a local hospital.

___Find a local organization to which you can volunteer your time.

___Volunteer at Special Olympics, Habitat for Humanity, state parks, hospitals, senior citizen centers, environmental organizations, political campaigns, etc.

___Other ______________________________

___Other ______________________________

___Other ______________________________

___Other ______________________________

___Other ______________________________

___Other ______________________________

Giving Back

FOR THE FACILITATOR

I. Purpose

To embrace diversity through altruistic actions.

II. General Comments

Teens evaluate options to decide which activities best match their interests and talents.

III. Possible Activities

a. Write *Give* on the board and ask about things that are given (money, time, effort, expertise, support, care or material gifts, etc.).

b. Write *Give Back* and ask its meaning (to give to someone or something because you received gifts).

c. Ask teens to brainstorm gifts they have received (they will probably mention material goods).

d. Prompt teens to identify gifts they may have overlooked (food, shelter, clothing, health).

e. Prompt teens to identify gifts they have received that did not cost the giver money (love, care, compassion, guidance).

f. Prompt teens to identify their gifts that they can give to others (ability, talent, time, care).

g. Distribute the *Giving Back* handout; a volunteer reads the instructions and rating system aloud.

h. Allow time for completion.

i. Encourage teens to share their responses and to explain their ratings.

j. Direct teens who rated the same items with a number 1 (GREAT IDEA) to form teams and develop action plans.

Examples

- Teens who want to offer their musical talents can go as a group to a skilled care facility.
- Teens interested in movie donations can make flyers and design collection bins to distribute around school.
- In each team a writer will note: *Who? What? When? Where? How?*

k. The group re-convenes and writers share their teams' action plans.

l. Ideally the activities will be completed within a specific time frame (one month or whatever applies).

m. Follow up with teams doing a *Show and Tell* with photos if appropriate to highlight their events.

IV. Enrichment Activities

a. Ask teens to brainstorm additional ways to give back to the universe.

b. Encourage teens to form a *Giving Back Club.*

- Recruit students from other classes or schools.
- Take turns rotating through activities and organizations.
- Publish a monthly newsletter.
- Create a multi-media display of the club's activities to share ideas and enlist more assistance from community businesses.

It's Your Turn to Teach

Carefully Taught
Lyrics by Oscar Hammerstein II

"You've got to be taught to hate and fear;
you've got to be taught from year to year;
it's got to be drummed in your dear little ear;
you've got to be carefully taught.

You've got to be taught to be afraid
of people whose eyes are oddly made,
and people whose skin is a different shade;
you've got to be carefully taught.

You've got to be taught before it's too late;
before you are six or seven or eight,
to hate all the people your relatives hate;
you've got to be carefully taught.

You've got to be carefully taught!"

1. Plan a fun class to teach young children the actual intention of Mr. Hammerstein (how family and environment can influence people to either accept and include, or hate and fear, people of a different culture).

2. Present your lesson to your classmates.

3. How can you *take your show on the road?*

It's Your Turn to Teach

FOR THE FACILITATOR

I. Purpose

To enhance awareness of messages that influence teens to be prejudiced against people from other cultures.

II. General Comments

By teaching young children to accept and embrace diversity, teens adopt the ideas themselves.

III. Possible Activities

a. If possible have a white board, dry erase markers, plain paper and crayons available.

b. Encourage a discussion about teens' favorite musicals.

c. Explain that teens will analyze lyrics from the play and movie, *South Pacific.*

d. Distribute the *It's Your Turn to Teach* handout and ask a volunteer to read the lyrics aloud.

e. Ask teens to interpret the song (responses will vary).

f. Ask teens from whom prejudice is learned (family/care providers, friends, the media, etc.).

g. Brainstorm ways teens could present the opposite message to young children.
Possibilities
- Create an illustrated story book.
- Present a chalk talk (a monologue presentation while the speaker draws on the board).
- Perform a short play.
- Compose a poem about acceptance with accompanying movements that children can copy.

h. Ask teens what types of characters would appeal to young children.
Possibilities
- Children
- Animals
- Aliens
- Robots
- Super Heroes
- Toys that come to life (dolls, teddy bears, etc.)

i. Encourage teens to work in teams; a writer lists their ideas on the handout.

j. Alternatively teens work individually to record their ideas.

k. Allow time for teams or individuals to prepare their story books or rehearse for a chalk talk, play, etc.

l. Ask teens to take turns reading their story books aloud as they would to a group of children, presenting their chalk talks, poems with movements, skits, etc.

m. Encourage a discussion of other ways teens can influence younger siblings, children for whom they babysit, etc.

n. Discuss ways teens could *take their shows on the road.*
Possibilities
- Photocopy and distribute their story books.
- Research the feasibility of presenting their lessons to elementary or pre-school-age children.
- Volunteer at a library or camp; present the lessons and involve children in related activities.

IV. Enrichment Activities

a. Explain that the Hammerstein lyrics were considered controversial and confrontational at the time.

b. Ask teens to debate whether storylines about race or ethnicity turn on, or turn away, audiences.

c. Encourage teens to plan lessons for peers similar to those they created for children.

Whole Person Associates is the leading publisher of training resources for professionals who empower people to create and maintain healthy lifestyles. Our creative resources will help you work effectively with your clients in the areas of stress management, wellness promotion, mental health and life skills.

Please visit us at our web site: **www.wholeperson.com**. You can check out our entire line of products, place an order, request our print catalog, and sign up for our monthly special notifications.

Whole Person Associates

800-247-6789

